Susan Barnard,

D0899660

BROKEN ALABASTER BOX

BY RENITA HOOF

My Prayer is that you Will be inspired by my scars !

Renita H. Hoof

Broken Alabaster Box
Copyright © 2017 by Renita M. Hoof
**We want to hear from you. Please send your comments about this
book to: renita.hoof1972@yahoo.com
To contact the author or book an event, please email:
renita.hoof1972@yahoo.com or call 501-247-7715**
Cover Design - ISpeak Publishing Service
Interior Design - ISpeak Publishing Service
Publishing Service-ISpeak Publishing Service
Editing - Make It Plain Ministries

All rights reserved. No part of this book may be reproduced, stored
in a retrieved system, or transmitted in any form or by any means,
electronic, mechanical, photocopying, recording, scanning, or
otherwise, without the prior written permission of the author.

All Scriptures come from:
Basic English Bible (BEB)
English Standard Version (ESV)
King James Version (KJV)
Living Bible (TLB)
New International Version (NIV)
New King James Version (NKJV)
New Living Translation (NLT)

Disclaimer

All the material contained in this book is provided for educational and informational purposes only. No responsibility can be taken for any results or outcomes resulting from the use of this material. While every attempt has been made to provide information that is both accurate and effective, the author does not assume any responsibility for the accuracy or use/misuse of this information.

Printed in the United States of America

ISBN 978-06920639-03

ISBN 0692063900

ISpeak Publishing Service

Tiffany M. Moorer, CEO

email: ispeakpublishing@gmail.com

Little Rock, AR.

501-519-6996

ACKNOWLEDGMENTS

To my Savior, JESUS CHRIST:

I dedicate this book to You first and foremost. Without Your direction, I would be lost. You have always been there for me – even when You seemed far off. You never left me nor forsook me. The times I thought You were unavailable were the times I found You to be the closest. When I was in the pit, You were there. In the palace, You are there. It was when I was in my deepest, darkest sinful place when I came to know You as my GOD, my secret keeper, my forgiver and my restorer. I love You, Jehovah!

To my dearest husband, Nicholas T. Hoof:

You have been by my side through tumultuous times and have believed in me when I didn't believe in myself: The thought of moving mountains and walking on water was never an issue for you. You always believed I could do anything except fail. Your endless prayers for me have always kept me balanced, and for that I thank you! You are my friend and my confidant. Words can't express how thankful I am to have you on this journey with me.

To my firstborn, my son, David, Jeremiah James Jackson:

You have been my "ride or live" for many years. You were there in the struggle and there in the good times. I have always believed in you and your ability to lead so many to The Lord. You have an internal calming leadership quality that will have many following you to CHRIST. Don't ever change lane … stay on the path on which He is leading you, and you never will go wrong. You are greatness!

To my beautiful daughter, my "Deborah," Victory Marie-Divine Jackson:

You have wisdom beyond your years. GOD has gifted you with favor from an early age. He has anointed your voice to sing as well as to speak His Word. Do not *ever* turn to the left or the right – always keep your eyes on the Prize. GOD has anointed you for such a time as this. Your journey will be different from that of your brother; however, it will still be the same. GOD has named you Victory, so remember, in everything you say and do, to give Him all the praise and the glory forever and ever. He is going to blow your mind with all the doors He opens for you.

To both my children, don't ever forget about each other. Stay connected. Have each other's back. Love each other. Don't let anything come between you all. Grow together. Never leave or forsake one another. You both are World Changers; never forget that!

To my parents, Charles and Dorothy Harrison:

Words can't express how grateful I am to have had two parents in the household.

Daddy, you showed me what a *real* husband looks like. You were consistent with a voice of authority. It was my pleasure to care for you before you went home to be with The Lord. I think of you so often, and my eyes fill with tears when I do. I would not take back one day of being with you through your illnesses. Holding your hand and fighting beside you will always be one of the proudest moments of my life. You always believed in me and thought I could change the world. Well, Daddy, this is my first step toward that end.

My dearest Mother, when I was younger I always wanted to be like you – confident and fierce! I wanted to command attention when I walked into a room, just as you did. I watched you raise three children alone during most of our young lives. I watched you dismiss relationships that weren't conducive with what you were teaching us as children. You were a trendsetter who didn't take no for an answer. If you believed in something, you would stand by it to the end. You set goals and accomplished them no matter how strong the current that was pushing against you. You taught me these values, which I taught my children, and for that I say thank you. Regardless of what we have been through, you still are the best mother that has ever walked the face of this earth. I pray many blessings for you.

To Bishop and Mother D.L. Lindsey:

Your lives have given me life and hope as I continue this journey with my husband and children. You are so inspirational. The encouragement and wisdom you have imparted are priceless. I thank you for loving GOD unconditionally and allowing me to see what a real sermon looks like.

To Pastor and First Lady Allen as well as my Worship Center Church of God in Christ Family:

I am at awe of what GOD is doing in this season. I am thankful to be able to walk among such spiritual giants. You all sharpen me and make me better each day. GOD is going to add to the church to the point that there will not be enough room to contain everyone. You all are amazing, and we haven't seen anything yet!

To Jackie Snider and Family: Thank you for being the protector of your little sister. Even though there was a time where we were distant, I want you to know that no one could ever take your place. I have one *real* sister, and that's you, "crazy" and all. I love you!

To my Little Big Brother, Bishop Jay Johnson and Family: I love you, too! You are one to be admired and looked up to. I am very proud of you. You are an awesome dad, husband and man of GOD. The sky is the limit for you and your ministry.

To my entire Burris Family: I observed you showing silent patience and standing in the balance as I grew from a "Peanut" to an adult. You have loved me as the only child of my biological father. You never treated me as if I were a mistake. Aunt Mary, you took me in when I was an obstinate teenager, allowing me to grow into a full woman … flaws and all. For that, I want to say thank you! TJ and Trell, you shared your mom with me when you all were struggling yourselves and she was trying to be your mother and father. I want to say "thank you" to the both of you as well. Aunt Paula, Shirley, Nita, I love you sooo much. Thank you for being such a great support.

To Lois Burris, my "Muddear": I took it for granted that you would always be around. How foolish I was to think this! I dream about you often and watch you running toward the glory of The Lord in those dreams. I miss you with every fiber of my being. You would be so proud of me. Thank you for showing me how to forgive others, even when I suffer the unthinkable at their hands. I will always love you!

To Daddy Floyd: I never got a chance to meet you, and no one really talked about you much, but I was told you were strong and resilient. I'm sorry that your life was taken early ... only GOD knows the whole story. I would like to believe that you know I turned out all right. I love you, Daddy, even if you never got a chance to hear me say it. – Your Little Peanut

To my gifted editor, Helaine R. Williams of Make it Plain Ministries: I want to especially thank you. Your expertise made this process so much easier than I ever expected. Words can't express my appreciation.

To my publisher, Tiffany Greene-Moorer of ISpeak Publishing Company: You took my vision and expressed it beautifully.

To the readers of *Broken Alabaster Box*: This book is for you! For me to be this transparent was very painful; however, it was necessary. I use my trials to encourage you and let you know you can make it, no matter what the circumstance. My prayer is that you will grow from this and come to the understanding that GOD is able to do the exceeding and the abundant in your life. I love each of you!

ENCOURAGEMENT FOR THE AUTHOR

In this book, Renita Hoof shares her hurts, griefs and disappointments. The enemy thought it was over, but God brought her through; He left her here to tell her story. She is a survivor! Renita's life has been one that is dedicated to her Lord. Her testimony is, "If you can stand the pull, God's love will pull you through." This book will not only inspire, but give one hope.

– Bishop and Mother D.L. Lindsey

For the past several years, I have observed your spiritual growth and character transformation. It has been a humbling experience to watch you morph into the Godly woman you have become. Your presence alone exudes the bright light of God's glory and the commitment of His mercy. Every life obstacle that you have publicly overcome is inspiring to all who know you. Your ongoing story is not only proof of God's amazing grace but a platform for promising hope. God bless you as you bless others!

– Pastor Lloyd W. Allen III

Evangelist Renita Hoof is a powerful and anointed woman who exhibits a unique style of delivery while ministering the Word of God. I am confident that the book *Broken Alabaster Box* is a work of inspiration and true transparency, released from an upcoming voice in the Kingdom of God.

– Pastor Alvin Coleman Jr.

You are someone I call my ride or life, my friend, my first love, someone I can depend on. You have been there through every loose tooth, bad grade, good grade, runny nose, sorrow and so forth. You have established the foundation of Jesus Christ in Jay's and my lives, and for that I am forever grateful. I have seen you behind the scenes for 15 years, and now God has granted you the platform to share your testimony in book form. The magnitude of the people who are going to find healing and answers in this book is so great, I'm honestly nervous for you. However, the Lord promised to never leave your side. You are highly remarkable. Never forget that. Oh, and guess what, Mom? I love you.

– Victory Marie-Divine Jackson

No one is more qualified to write about brokenness and restoration than you. I have seen you, during your brokenness, continue to trust God, pray to God and praise Him. Because of this, the oil of restoration and peace continually flows through your spirit, blessing all that's hurting and needy. I pray that you will continue to obey God, and in doing so experience "the greater" that He has for you! Love you!

– Donna Lindsey Robinson

"A friend loveth at all times, and a brother (sister) is born for adversity." – Proverbs 17:17

If you're fortunate enough in life, you will find that one special friend. That one person who changes your life, just by being a part of it. Someone who loves you when you're hard to love, believes in you when you don't believe in yourself, who listens to you when you don't have a voice, and who fights with you and for you in adversity.

I am forever indebted to God for sending me my forever friend, my mentor, my midwife, my SISTER! Your testimony and transparency are destined to change the lives of countless others. You survived, you persevered, and you were BORN for such a time as this!

– *Kaneisha Campbell*

For if you remain silent at this time, relief and deliverance for the Jews will arise from another place. And who knows but that you have come to your royal position for such a time as this?" (Esther 4:14, NIV)

In a day and society where most are reluctant to say what needs to be said ...where most are more concerned with their image than their testimony ... GOD HAS CALLED YOU TO BE A VOICE.

In a day and society where most are talking behind the scenes, often sharing views and opinions; when few are out front sharing their words as a tool to build, encourage, and restore, GOD HAS CALLED YOU TO BE A VOICE.

In a day and society where transparency is invisible, and hiding is more prevalent than helping, GOD HAS CALLED YOU TO BE A VOICE.

God has placed you where you are for such a time as this. Use what He has put into you to bring life to those around you. Be encouraged and write until there is nothing more to say.

– *Elder Julius DeBerry*

FOREWORD

Renita Hoof is a woman I have watched very closely since the day I was born. I have seen her at her best, I have seen her at her worst, and she is the same person through and through. Her faith in the Lord is truly her greatest strength and has brought her farther than I could imagine. She is a woman of God and walks with dignity and grace.

Renita is a natural leader. This has been proven by how swiftly she has moved through the ranks at her job and in the church. The anointing on her is powerful. She speaks and preaches the Word with conviction; the Holy Spirit is brought forth with her every message. People gravitate toward her. But she is quick to remind everyone that all glory goes to God, and that nothing she does is possible without Him.

Throughout the years I have watched her go through trial after trial, tribulation after tribulation. Her method of dealing with those trials and tribulations has stayed the same: an unrelenting faith in God and an unwillingness to give up. She is truly a warrior in the Army of the Lord. Her strength in her brokenness and her humility is beautiful to behold. She has a way of picking up the pieces any time they fall. She strives to offer her Lord that perfect alabaster box, even while broken.

Renita's love for God and willingness to do his work is what birthed this book. She is not a natural-born writer, so this is truly a work done by Jesus through her. She is a saint of the highest order and woman of the highest stature. I honor her.

– Jeremiah J. Jackson

TABLE OF CONTENTS

Acknowledgments...v

Encouragement for the Author...xi

Foreword...xv

Introduction...19

Chapter 1: I may not understand, but GOD is Faithful.............23

Chapter 2: The Struggle of the Process.....................................39

Chapter 3: Positioned for Persecution.......................................59

Chapter 4: Stay in the Fight...73

Chapter 5: Reaching for Better by Faith...................................85

Chapter 6: Perfecting Your Faith..95

Chapter 7: Love Covers All..103

Chapter 8: Called to be New...111

Chapter 9: Keeping it Real, Not Safe..125

Chapter 10: GOD's Timing..133

Bibliography...151

About the Author..153

INTRODUCTION

*And one of the Pharisees desired him that
he would eat with him. And he went into the
Pharisee's house, and sat down to meat. And,
behold, a woman in the city, which was a
sinner, when she knew that Jesus sat at meat
in the Pharisee's house, brought an alabaster
box of ointment, And stood at his feet behind
him weeping, and began to wash his feet with
tears, and did wipe them with the hairs of
her head, and kissed his feet, and anointed
them with the ointment. Now when the Pharisee which had bidden him saw it, he spake
within himself, saying, This man, if he were
a prophet, would have known who and what
manner of woman this is that toucheth him:
for she is a sinner ... And [JESUS] turned to
the woman, and said unto Simon, Seest thou
this woman? I entered into thine house, thou
gavest me no water for my feet: but she hath
washed my feet with tears, and wiped them
with the hairs of her head. Thou gavest me no
kiss: but this woman since the time I came in
hath not ceased to kiss my feet. My head with
oil thou didst not anoint: but this woman hath
anointed my feet with ointment. Wherefore I
say unto thee, Her sins, which are many, are*

*forgiven; for she loved much: but to whom
little is forgiven, the same loveth little. And he
said unto her, Thy sins are forgiven.*

Luke 7:36-39; 44-48 (KJV)

The Biblical story of the woman with the alabaster box had a major impact on me. I will go into her story later in the book, but I will say now that I once considered myself even lower than this woman, who had committed many sins, who was considered the lowest of the low ... but whose desire to honor JESUS, in her own humble way, drove her to disregard not just the social protocol of the day but others' opinion of her. She honored JESUS by anointing His feet with expensive perfume contained in an alabaster box.

We all have an alabaster box that we can present to the LORD ... our submitted selves, forged in praise and worship and, being assured of His forgiveness, completed in obedience. No sins are too great or too numerous for us to present our alabaster box. But I went through so much, and felt so debased, that I considered my box to be broken, its contents spilled and irretrievable.

I never imagined I would be an author, so I was shocked at the prophesy. I didn't do well in school as I am a hands-on type of person, a hard worker but not very analytical ... basically a B/C student. I certainly didn't do well in English, so writing a book was the last thing on my mind. I'd wanted to attend college badly; however, my grades did not attract a scholarship and my parents told me they could not afford to send me to higher education. The things I did have going for me were drive, determination and will. I also had a love for JESUS, instilled by my parents at a young age. They taught me that I couldn't go wrong with loving

Him. This foundation helped me to get through some unthinkable times in my life.

But I was shocked at what I was told by a pastor by the name of Alvin Coleman. He'd been invited to my home church, The Worship Center Church of GOD in Christ (COGIC) for our Passion Week revival, which took place April 9-11, 2017. During this revival, Pastor Coleman prophesied that I would write three books.

I remember the times the Lord would give me a Word to pray for others whom He had called to write a book. My spiritual baby would leap inside of me as if to confirm that this was a Word for me as well! I would always shake it off, however, as I have always doubted myself when it comes to writing.

When Pastor Coleman prophesied over me, I remember rolling on the floor, my spirit battling with my flesh as to whether this prophecy was real. I remember thinking, *Pastor Coleman must have me confused with my best friend who has a master's degree and who is very intelligent. He certainly can't have the correct person! She is an amazing person with an overpowering ministry and an anointing on her life that is indescribable; every word that seems to be prophesied is for her... surely he has me confused with her!* You see, I am usually the background person ... the midwife, never the wife. Those who *think* they know me would say this is not a true statement because of my personality. But those who *really* know me know this is how I perceive myself.

It took several months from the time of this for me to begin this journey, as I still did not believe GOD would use me to inspire His people through the writings of a book.

This book, as well as the other two to come, are birthed out of sickness. I fell sick for several days, and the doctors were unable to tell me what was wrong with me. GOD has a way of getting the attention of those He loves! Let me be clear; He did not cause the illness. However, healing and strength comes through obedience. Whatever our need is, we must be obedient and watch Him be faithful over His Word. He watches over it to perform it (Jeremiah 1:12).

My next two books have me excited as well. They will be titled *Raising David and Deborah* and *Blessed Beyond Your Brokenness*. I know GOD is going to bring healing and restoration to all broken places for so many women through the transparency of these books.

I must be honest. These books will take you into your secret places, places where doors have been shut that you never thought would open again. These are places you hid from others and harbored secrets you have wanted to forget. GOD is going to heal your scars and bring things to light that He will cleanse and wipe away!

This debut book, meanwhile, is from the heart of a woman who has been broken, abused, molested, raped, betrayed, neglected…. a woman who has committed adultery, along with other carnal sins … but who still has enough bandwidth to believe GOD for the impossible. You will read of my tragedies as well as my triumph.

I am so excited to share my life story with you, and I pray you will be inspired to continue this journey with JESUS. It so worth it!

Chapter 1

I may not understand, but GOD is Faithful

†

Man [or woman] that is born of a woman is of few days and full of trouble.

Job 14:1, KJV

As I look back over my life, I can see the times I have failed to understand the wisdom and knowledge of GOD. However, I have always found Him to be faithful … especially during the most difficult times in my life.

I grew up in Little Rock, Arkansas. My younger brother, older sister and I were raised by my mother and adoptive father, who my mother married when I was 11 or 12 years old. My biological father had passed before I was born. I was told that my uncle, my mother's brother, shot and killed him. Rumor has it that my dad was very stout and strong. From what I understand, people feared him, so when the altercation between my uncle and my father occurred, the result was that I was never afforded the opportunity to see my father's face, or hear his voice. I have seen only one picture of my father. I haven't really heard that much about him; I am sure the tragedy was very painful for all involved, including both sets of my grandparents. Both lost their sons, and I lost my daddy, on that fateful winter day. I had a crack in my alabaster box before I was even born.

My parents were very hands-on and quite strict, especially as my adoptive father had been in the military. They always taught us to make our own decisions, rather than acting on the decisions of others. The only whipping my dad ever gave me came when I was around 11 years old, after getting in trouble in school with one of my friends. He asked who got the idea for our behavior. I told him the truth: It was my friend's idea. He told me he was going to spank me good because I should never have allowed anyone to influence me to do wrong. He said that I was a leader and not a follower, and that I was to never forget that. That one statement changed my life … forever. It took root immediately. Deborah, the woman judge of Israel whose story was told in Judges 4-5, was being birthed in me. Allow me to talk a bit about being pregnant with purpose at birth.

We were pregnant with purpose before we were formed in the womb, before we were the proverbial twinkle in our parents' eyes. GOD knew us! We know this by John 15:16a, which says, "Ye have not chosen me, but I have chosen you, and ordained you, that ye should go and bring forth fruit, and that your fruit should remain ... " We know it by Jeremiah 1:5: "Before I formed thee in the belly I knew thee; and before thou camest forth out of the womb I sanctified thee, and I ordained thee a prophet unto the nations." And we know it by Psalm 139:15-16: "My substance (my embryo) was not hid from thee, when I was made in secret, and curiously wrought in the lowest parts of the earth. Thine eyes (O, Lord) did see my substance, yet being unperfect; and in thy book all my members were written, which in continuance were fashioned, when as yet there was none of them" (all KJV). Finally, Ephesians 1:11 tells us that "In Him we were also chosen, having been predestined according to the plan of Him who works out everything in conformity with the purpose of His will" (NIV).

Before it was documented at Ouachita County Hospital in Arkansas, where I was BORN, it was already documented in Heaven that I had purpose! Before I had life, GOD sent HIS LIFE to die on the Cross so that I could become pregnant with LIFE … a life made complete in JESUS CHRIST. Although I had cracks in my alabaster box, GOD was on the scene.

In my embryonic state, GOD called me and impregnated me with HIS purpose. But the moment I was birthed, an abortion order went out. Satan wanted to end this pregnancy. He wanted my lack of knowledge of really who I was and from Whom I came, to be my destination. He wanted bitterness in my heart. He wanted the weight of my father's and uncle's altercation to be on me, and tried to tell me the tragedy was my fault. He tried to abort my divine purpose in GOD, using such weapons as depression, failed relationships (I looked for love in all the wrong places), failed finances (I tried to buy happiness), sin, disappointments, fear, doubt – and even self-righteousness. Yes, I would go from one extreme to another, I was full of pride one day and full of doubt the next. To use John 10:10, the enemy has come to only kill, steal and destroy GOD's purpose. But JESUS tells us that He has come that we may have life and life more abundantly. He came so that we might bring forth GOD's purpose in the earth. And our main purpose is to tell, and show, a dying world that JESUS lives. When I think of the "GOD"ness of JESUS, I can't help but give Him praise for looking beyond my faults, sparing my purpose and delivering me from Satan's snares.

Granted, the pregnancy may bring birthing pains, problems, sleeplessness nights, failures and tears. But the good news is that "all things work together for good to them that love God, to them who are the called according to his purpose" (Romans 8:28. KJV). And "moreover whom he did predestinate, them he also called: and whom he called, them he also justified, and whom he justified, them he also glorified (Romans 8:30, also KJV).

Your pregnancy can get heavy and it can be difficult for you to push your purpose through. When it seems to take all that you have in you to continue, remember who your Father is. If you need provision in your pregnancy, call on Jehovah Jireh, your provider. When your pregnancy/purpose appears to have broken your body down, call on Jehovah Ra-pha, your healer. When everyone has left you, call on the name of Jehovah Shammah, your Lord who is present. When the devil tries to bring chaos on your purpose, call on Jehovah Shalom, your peace. When you need GOD's protection from the evil one, call on Jehovah Nissi, your banner.

Do this, and you'll find truth in Habakkuk 2:3 (KJV): "For the vision [purpose] is yet for an appointed time, but at the end it shall speak and not lie; though it tarry, wait for it; because it will surely come, it will not tarry."

Satan's abortion attempt

The first of the devil's attacks on my purpose was the identity crisis from which I spent my childhood suffering. Many of us are familiar with the New Testament parable of the talents, I remember comparing myself to the person who received only one talent. Everyone else I knew, it seemed, had received two or more talents. I knew people who could sing, praise dance, quote scriptures *and* preach! I remember convincing myself that I didn't have to have the multiple talents or gifts that others had. Being a member was all that I was called to do, I concluded, and I would just have to accept that.

These thoughts led me into depression, jealousy and self-doubt … cracks in my alabaster box. I would look around the room at work and at church and see gifts, talent and intelligence to my left and to my right, but I didn't realize my own self-worth. Little did I know that if those with one talent would simply allow GOD to work that talent, He will anoint it to endless possibilities in Him. We just need to remember to "work the one!"

My realization of this came at the end of a long road, however … a road potholed by the strongholds I dealt with that stemmed from the rape I suffered at a young age, and the resulting destruction of my self-esteem. (I will get more into that as we take this journey together.)

I had friends in high school who were much prettier and smarter than I, or so I thought. It wasn't until recently that I realized that beauty and wisdom come from GOD and within. Ecclesiastes 2:26a shows that "to the person who pleases Him, GOD gives wisdom, knowledge and happiness," whereas, 1 Peter 3:3-4 reveals that "Your beauty should not come from outward adornment, such as elaborate hairstyles and the wearing of gold jewelry or fine clothes. Rather, it should be that of your inner self, the unfading beauty of a gentle and quiet spirit, which is of great worth in GOD's sight." (NIV)

Depression came easy to me; it was a comfort zone. It caused me to go into the darkest places and isolate myself from the world. When I was depressed, I didn't see myself as GOD did. I saw myself as talentless and useless. Even today, I have to pull down thoughts that try to exalt themselves above the knowledge of what GOD has called me to be.

When I didn't know or understand GOD, I didn't think He was

faithful. I didn't think He could be touched by my infirmities. I didn't have a relationship with Him; therefore, I didn't know how to worship Him in the true spirit of holiness. I didn't know how to worship Him, period. It was from the scars in my life, however, that a true foundation was built.

In Matthew 16:13-20, JESUS asked the disciples, "Who do men say that I, the Son of Man, am?"

They replied, "Some say John the Baptist, others say Elijah, and still others say Jeremiah." JESUS responded, "But who do YOU say that I am?" Simon Peter answered, "You are the Messiah, the Son of the living GOD."

JESUS replied, "Blessed are you, Simon son of Jonah, for this was not revealed to you by flesh and blood, but by my Father in heaven. And I tell you that you are Peter, and on this rock I will build my church, and the gates of hell shall not prevail against it."

Now if you remember, Peter was the disciple who denied JESUS, the disciple who had a "hot mouth" … the disciple who had a temper and who, most of the time, took risks. But here we read that JESUS still declared that Peter was blessed and that He would build His church through Peter's revelation. Despite all of Peter's flaws and shortcomings, JESUS saw past that – and still called him blessed!

We are all like Peter. We have had some of the same issues Peter had. As far as I've come in the Lord, I still must pray against those issue-causing spirits. I have come to realize that as long as I am in this fleshly body, I must depend on GOD to help me … with me.

I think this is what is so unappetizing to nonbelievers. We as

Christians don't like to testify about the things from which GOD has delivered us. Our outward appearance fools the naked and untrained spiritual eye to think that we are flawless and never made mistakes. But I am here to tell you that we all have fallen short of the glory of GOD and will continue to make mistakes as long as we live. Therefore, brand-new mercies are afforded us every day.

What I began to recognize is that I had allowed my circumstances to rename me and redefine who I was called to be. I didn't understand why, as a young child, I was being touched inappropriately by my cousin. I knew it was wrong, but I didn't know what to do about it, or who to tell. I was afraid at first. Then it became the normal thing, something I expected to happen. It birthed something in me … a spirit of lust, if you would. I was so young, I didn't know what lust was. But it caused me to go from one grandparent's house, where I was being touched, to another grandparent's house, where I tried to touch another cousin in the same manner. Thank GOD for JESUS! An aunt came in, caught me and punished me, after which I never did that again. But as a 5-year-old girl, I was only repeating what had been done to me.

As I grew older, I realized that my mother was always trying to protect my siblings and me from the bad things of the world. She would never allow us to stay overnight at our friends' houses, for instance, because of her fear of what we could get into. She would send us to her parents' house for the summer, thinking we were safe. But how many people know that the devil waits patiently for whom he seeks to destroy? It was while I was visiting my grandparents that a female cousin touched me inappropriately. It was one of the most horrible experiences in my life. It was a setup by the enemy! I asked myself, *How and why could this happen?* Again, I was so young; I had no one to turn to.

I didn't understand. But I would soon find out that GOD is faithful.

I was about 10 years old, growing up in a Caucasian church where we played the bells instead of serving in the Sunshine band (a version of children's church in my current denomination, the Church of God in Christ). During service one day, the Pastor opened the doors of the church for all those who would come and accept CHRIST and receive salvation. I will never forget the pull on my heart that morning. I went to the altar and gave my life to CHRIST. I immediately fell in love with this Man … this Man that I felt was going to be with me always. I knew my life was never going to be the same after that moment. JESUS came into my life and began a work in me, the manifestation of which I am now seeing today.

I can't say that life was easier after that day. It became a distant memory once I entered my teenage years. Don't get me wrong; I knew CHRIST was still with me. However, it was a long time before I again felt Him like I did the day I accepted Him.

Fast-forward to ninth grade and the day I lied to my mom, telling her I had a volleyball game. I didn't. I went to a friend's house to meet up with my boyfriend while she met up with hers. Mind you, I wasn't supposed to have a boyfriend. I wasn't yet 16, and my parents were very strict. But, being young, naive and disobedient, I rebelled.

Once we all met at the house, the four of us retreated to my friend's bedroom for what I thought would just be kissing. I never expected to be taken advantage of … and not in a million years did I expect the unthinkable to happen. My boyfriend and I, along with my friend and her boyfriend, lay across the bed kissing. In what seemed like a split second, my boyfriend ripped my pants zipper, pulled down my panties and penetrated me ... while my friend's boyfriend held me down by my arms. Thank GOD, I was a champion sprinter with very strong abdomen and leg strength. With all my might, I flipped my boyfriend over my head with my legs.

The damage had been done, however, and it was horrific. Blood was everywhere, my clothes were ripped and stained and I was crying profusely. Throughout all this my best friend stood back and watched. She never lifted a finger to defend me or even open her mouth in protest.

The next day at school was almost intolerable. I was humiliated because I thought everyone knew what happened to me; my boyfriend was a very popular athlete and was *proud* of what he had done! My friend and I never discussed the incident. (As I think back, I realize I used the word "friend" too loosely. She was never really my friend.) I could never tell my parents; I didn't want them to know their daughter was now "that" type of girl. My father would have been crushed. I loved him too much to disappoint him.

I didn't understand, but I would soon find out that GOD is faithful.

I began to feel like David's daughter Tamar did in II Samuel 13 in the Old Testament. She had to live as a "desolate woman" (v. 20) with the shame of being taken advantage of. She had to live with a secret she could not divulge. She could not look in the mirror and see the same person she saw before the rape. She had to lock this tragedy into that secret place in her mind. This is what I did. I locked these painful experiences up in a secret mental lockbox, never to be revealed … or so I thought. They were the cracks in my alabaster box.

These experiences began to reshape me, as well as haunt me. I became angry and distant. My grades suffered. I was an athlete before this encounter, but afterward, I gave that up. Depression was my first name and low self-esteem was my garment.

I trained myself to put things away in that mental lockbox. If I encountered anything that was difficult to handle, I would just tell myself, *Lock it away. Forget it. Don't think about it. Don't bring it up. It never happened.* This tactic worked for many years until I began to realize that it was causing different voices – different personalities, if you will – to manifest in my mind and in my life.

An insatiable desire to be successful has always run in my veins. I wanted to be "somebody." I wanted a husband, two kids and a dog; a nice home with a picket fence; and a nice car. I wanted the images that the world set before me on television and in magazines. I was bound and determined to be successful. The problem was my lack of close role models for this standard of success. The one person in my family who came close to what I considered successful was my mother, and I wanted to be just like her: beautiful, strong, determined and resilient.

As part of my plan to become that "somebody" I wanted to go to college. As I approached my high-school graduation with what would barely be a 3.0 grade point average, I went to my parents with the news that I had been accepted into one of the nearby colleges. I was so very excited … but that excitement was short-lived. My parents told me they would not be able to send me to college as they did not have the money.

I was devastated and deflated. I had no idea, at that point, what I was going to do. My friends were preparing for college – receiving scholarship information, having celebratory gatherings, shopping for dorm-room décor – while I was falling into a deep depression, having no idea what I was going to do and where I was going to end up.

I couldn't understand, but the one thing that I did know was that GOD was faithful.

I ultimately decided that if I couldn't enter college, I would enter the military. Internal strength began to build within me as I drove to the United States Army recruiting office, in Little Rock, where I found myself filling out paperwork to enlist in the Army Reserve, alone. *Oh my goodness,* I remember thinking. *What am I doing? I am the most girly girl there is. Why would I ever enroll in the military?* Oh yeah, because I was bound and determined to be successful! I wanted that house with the white picket fence and the two kids and the nice car, plus the dog. (The husband, at this point, had become optional.)

Meanwhile, my relationship with my parents had become strained. I was angry because things did not work out as I had hoped. I felt let down by my parents, who I felt should have planned for my education and, therefore, my future. If I had known what I know now, I would have been rejoicing instead of being angry. I would have been thanking them for the JESUS that they had instilled in me all those years they dragged me and my siblings to church. I should have been mad at *myself* for my failure to do a better job of preparing for my own future. But of course, it was my parents' fault instead of mine. *I should not have to join the military,* I grumbled. *I should have been going to college like the rest of my friends.* But join the military I did.

After successfully completing basic training and AIT (Advanced Individual Training) for becoming a surgical technologist – surprisingly, graduating at the top of my class – I felt that I had found my purpose, what I was born to do ...or so I thought. It seemed as if I was born to work in the operating room, assisting surgeons with some of the most difficult operations known to man. After my military training was complete, I received my first operating-room job. It was the early 1990s; I was a 19-year-old making more than $30,000 a year, more money than most. I was well on my way to becoming that successful, relevant person; well on my way to having the American Dream. Nothing could stop me now … right?

 Little did I know that I was in for a rude awakening, with many disappointments to follow. Unfortunately, having achieved this bit of success, I'd long forgotten the JESUS Who had given it to me. I'd left Him at in the barracks at Fort Sam Houston, where I many nights I asked Him to help me pass anatomy, microbiology and physiology as well as endure the rigorous physical demands of the military. I forgot about how I'd premeditated shooting myself in the leg to keep from being deployed during Operation Desert Storm, the Gulf War. But the Lord gave me the strength not to go through with maiming myself … and I was not deployed after all.

I'd left JESUS at graduation. I'd forgotten to pack Him up and bring Him back home with me, and after all, I was becoming successful. The American Dream was in sight.

Growing up, I hadn't been allowed to go to parties. So, when I did get a taste of adult freedom, it blew my mind. While in the military I partied every weekend, traveling from state to state to do so. Now I never saw my parents drink or smoke – never saw them be irresponsible, actually – so when I partied, I never drank or smoked; these habits were not a part of my regimen. Staying out all night certainly was, however. I also found myself looking for love in all the wrong places. This is when the dream that I'd held closely began to slip through my fingers.

Leaving a difficult relationship, I quit my well-paying job and moved back to my small hometown, where there was one hospital and several clubs. At this point, the clubs were the only thing that I was interested in. The job was a no-brainer. I could deliver babies, assist with colon resections and do a craniotomy with my eyes closed. *I got this*, I used to think. *No one can do this better than me.* I worked in that small hospital during the day and partied at night. I had the home, the nice car, another relationship, and a dog. At this point, I'd decided against the kids; they would only get in the way. I had arrived, or so I thought. But, again, I'd left JESUS at Fort Sam Houston and hadn't really thought about Him since.

The harder I worked, the more partying I did. I rewarded myself with clothes, shoes, car accessories, furniture, and diamonds. I wanted it all. I *had* it all. All except JESUS. But that was perfectly fine to me at the time because it appeared as if I really didn't need Him. I knew He was real. I believed in Him still; I just didn't *need* Him anymore. I could take it from here. No need in bothering Him with what I could take care of myself.

But Proverbs 16:18 says, "Pride goes before destruction, a haughty spirit before a fall" (NIV). The enemy was waiting.

The more I partied, the more my job performance was adversely affected. I called in two to three times out of the week, making up every story I could think of to try to convince my boss that she should allow me to take an off-day. Needless to say, the job did not last long. My boss finally took me aside and told me I was not carrying my load; my teammates were carrying it for me. I was so pride-filled, I decided to quit. I didn't want anyone carrying anything for me.

The one thing I'd forgotten to do before quitting was count the costs of doing so. Again, there was only one hospital in town and surgical technology was all I had been trained to do. (It really fit what I was *called* to do: help to heal other people's brokenness.)

I quickly found myself in a predicament. I began to lose everything. I moved in with a cousin and began to invest in the illegal-drug trade. *I saw my uncle do it for years*, I told myself. *How hard could it be?* I took my last paycheck and had a so-called friend "flip" it for me, using it to obtain and sell drugs for me at a profit in exchange for a cut. I never saw the drugs or touched them myself; my friend handled them for me. *I had to do what I had to do,* I reasoned. *If selling drugs was how I was going to retain this dream, then selling was what it had to be.* My box was continuing to crack.

That arrangement didn't go well for long either, however. This so-called friend began to come back and tell me about one thing or another that had gone bad with my investment money and the transactions. The money dwindled until there was no more left.

I found myself broke, angry, defeated and depressed. *How could this have ever happened?* I wondered.

I also eventually found myself homeless. Everything I owned was in the trunk of my car. I would go to my friends' houses late in the afternoon, act like I was on my way somewhere, and conveniently fall asleep on their couches. I went from house to house, night after night, playing this game until these friends wised up and demanded that I contribute something for my stay. I quickly found out that one can't stay where one is not contributing.

Trying to find another job was a horrific experience. There was nothing else available in town except for a job in an industrial plant, and I knew I wasn't made to do that. I even put in several applications for janitorial work, but was denied.

Everything at this point was all wrong. I was so hungry I would go into grocery stores, open a product and eat it right there. I would go steal clothing from other stores. I was at rock bottom. Although I hadn't used drugs myself, I was in the same position as the people to whom I had indirectly sold drugs. The cracks in my alabaster box had multiplied.

I finally landed a job at a local gas station that sold food as well. At this point, I became a professional thief. I figured out a way to fill my gas tank and eat without being discovered. I hated myself for what I had become. I was a disgrace to myself ... 22 years old, living out of my car, stealing gas and food. There were so many things wrong with this picture. I couldn't figure out where I went wrong ... or so I tried to tell myself. I could have gone back home to my parents, but pride wouldn't let me. I could not let them know what a failure I had become.

I didn't understand, but I remembered that GOD is faithful. I hadn't stopped to call on Him yet, as I was embarrassed, ashamed and in disbelief. But soon I would find out that He is the Way, the Truth and the Life and without Him, there is no me.

Chapter 2

The Struggle of the Process

†

Since therefore Christ suffered in the flesh, arm yourselves
with the same way of thinking, for whoever has suffered in the
flesh has ceased from sin:

1 Peter 4, KJV

In my childhood, I really didn't understand what a process was. To me, it seemed that if there was an *action*, then there quickly had to be a *reaction*. After all, this is what I was taught in school – Newton's Third Law of Physics. No one ever taught me about "the process." I knew about the struggle, but not the process.

When we were very young, my mother did not have a car; we would catch the bus everywhere. The only time we would catch a cab would be during that one time of the month that we would go to the grocery store and buy lots of food with paper stamped-looking money. At that point, I really didn't realize that we were in a struggle. My mother never allowed us to think we were poor or that we didn't have what other children had. In fact, she did an excellent job keeping us sheltered from what other people thought of us; she did not allow their opinions to determine our destiny.

It was only when I visited friends and other family members that I realized yes, we were poor and yes, there was a struggle. It wasn't until I was older and living on my own that I realized what the struggle was. I certainly found out what self-inflicted struggles are. But more important, I found out about the process JESUS orchestrates in our lives. It's a simple process, but even the smartest people are bewildered by it. It's the process of love: "For God so loved the world, that he gave his only begotten Son, that whosoever believeth in him should not perish, but have everlasting life." (John 3:16, KJV)

One might assume that to love is simple, but how wrong we can be! You see, as children and even as adults, we are taught to love by *other people*. Or let me state it like this: Often we learn to love from how others love us. If we learn love as something that is not freely given as JESUS gave, then we give love out of necessity instead of as a matter of the heart.

Let me see if this makes more sense. Coming up, I never was told by my parents, or even my grandparents, that they loved me. Their love was shown by the food and shelter provided, but these words were never spoken. I also learned that every spanking was supposed to represent love, because this was what I was told; however, I didn't understand how pain could equate to love. As a result, if anyone gave me food and shelter – or hurt me – I would believe they loved me. This is *not* the message my parents and grandparents meant to send me, but this is what I conceptualized. This became my reality for many years. I began to live by the cracks in my alabaster box.

The Bible says in Job 1:6-7 that "one day the angels came to present themselves before the LORD, and Satan also came with them. The LORD said to Satan, 'Where have you come from?' Satan answered the LORD, "From roaming throughout the earth, going back and forth on it" (NIV). See, the enemy roams throughout the earth, going back and forth, seeking whom he may devour. He is very patient. He will wait for very long periods of time to carry out his plan to destroy GOD's people. In my case, Satan took the very thing my parents were trying to teach me about love, sustainability and discipline ... and flipped it to mean something wicked that would ultimately take me through a long, tumultuous process.

In so many ways, I was the Samaritan woman at the well about whom John so vividly wrote in Chapter 4 of his gospel. I was broken, depressed and downtrodden. There was nothing about me that I saw worth anything, except my body. I used it, because it worked. It worked to find love, shelter and food. I used it, because it helped me to find shelter, food and (I thought) love.

In John 4, traveling from Judea to Galilee, JESUS and his disciples came to Samaria. This was in the plan. The disciples had no idea, but JESUS had a date with a certain woman and He was not going to be late! This date was not a carnal date. This was a date with destiny that would cause this woman to interrupt her life and start a revolution in her hometown. She would become one of the first evangelists of the New Testament Scriptures.

It all began when a tired JESUS stayed and rested by Jacob's well as his disciples went to the village of Sychar to buy food. It was the hottest part of the day... a time people were usually in their homes staying out of the heat. Just as JESUS expected, the Samaritan woman – who'd had many men and was currently living "in sin" – chose this time to come draw water so that she could avoid the whispering and the dirty looks. After all, she knew who she was; she did not need anyone to tell her. She needed food and shelter like the next woman.

Well, JESUS, being JESUS, asked the woman to give Him a

drink of water.

"In His encounter with the woman at the well, JESUS broke three Jewish customs," writes Jack Zavada in "Woman at the Well - Bible Story Summary," at the website ThoughtCo.com. "First, he spoke to a woman; second, she was a Samaritan woman, a group the Jews traditionally despised; and third, he asked her to get him a drink of water, which would have made him ceremonially unclean from using her cup or jar."

Needless to say, the woman didn't understand why this Man would be asking her for a drink! "But you Jews do not deal with us Samaritans," she said. "How is it that you're asking ME for a drink?"

JESUS told the woman He could give her "living water" so that she would never thirst again. This piqued her interest, as she associated sustainability with love – which, remember, is what we all are looking for. JESUS used the words "living water" to refer to eternal life, the gift that would satisfy her soul's desire and which was only available through Him.

At first the Samaritan woman did not fully understand JESUS' meaning, as she was thinking of her need. Although they had never met in the natural realm, JESUS knew her in the spiritual realm ... even before she knew herself. In verses 15-18, He revealed that He knew she'd had five husbands and was now living with a man who was not her husband.

Then, JESUS began to speak to the broken places in this woman. He had her attention, because the pain of her past was playing on the projector of her mind: how she'd been told by each man in her past that she was the only thing that mattered to him, only to be let down and left desolate. How she quickly opened the door to another man, then another, then another … only for the same scenario to play out. How she was terrified at the thought of being married to her live-in lover because she was afraid the scenario she had lived so many times before would overtake her relationship with this man, too. How she bore the brunt of her community's scorn, agreeing in her heart with their conclusion that she was trash, she was nothing, and that her life would never change.

But JESUS now had her attention!

As she and JESUS talked about their two views on worship, the woman voiced her faith that a Messiah was coming. JESUS answered, "I who speak to you am He." (John 4:26).

"As the woman began to grasp the reality of her encounter with Jesus, the disciples returned," Zavada writes. "They were equally shocked to find him speaking to a woman." Especially this woman. A Samaritan woman. *What could she want from the Messiah?* they must have thought. *Was she trying to take advantage of Him?* I can imagine the self-righteous disdain in the eyes of the disciples … and the endless love in the eyes of the Father.

This is what I love about GOD. It doesn't matter what your background is. It doesn't matter what someone else thinks of you, nor does it matter what you think of yourself. What matters is what He thinks of you! GOD justifies and edifies. He uses the least of us to do His will, to advance His Kingdom. He loves using the unqualified, the broken and lost. If we could just change our perspective and stop our insecurities from taking root in our minds and overtaking our emotions, we can see ourselves as GOD sees us: sons and daughters of the King. Royalty.

The now-transformed woman took the first step in re-establishing her identity ... that of an evangelist, the bearer of Good News to her townspeople: "Come, see a man who told me all that I ever did. Can this be the Christ?" (John 4:29, ESV)

When this unnamed woman ... Wait. Think about that phrase for a moment. *Unnamed woman.*

This is where *revelation* comes in, rather than *relevance*. In my life, I desired a name for myself. Oftentimes, in the secular world, we are not that successful. We have degrees and careers that look like everyone else's, so there is no uniqueness, nothing that makes us special, nothing that grabs attention. Sad to say, we bring those same narcissistic ways into the church. We as Christians want to make a name or a brand for ourselves, so we start to celebritize our Kingdom work. We make it about *us*. We aren't satisfied with being known merely as "the woman at the well." Noooo! We insist on being known as "Evangelist Sugar Foot Jones!"

When we take on this attitude, *we* get the glory and not GOD. As JESUS said in Matthew 6:2, our exaltation of ourselves is our only reward: "Therefore when thou doest thine alms, do not sound a trumpet before thee, as the hypocrites do in the synagogues and in the streets, that they may have glory of men. Verily I say unto you, They have their reward" (KJV).

As the Scripture goes, the Samaritan woman left her water pot and ran into the city, taking a chance at ridicule and mockery to tell the people to "come, see a Man" who could speak life to every broken place in their lives. She not only started a two-day revival in the city of Samaria; she started a revolution.

Because of this no-name woman, women all over the world can proclaim the goodness of JESUS. We can look past our yesterday and hope for tomorrow. We can believe that GOD has set a specific time to meet us where we are. We can trust that GOD is our secret-keeper and that He won't expose us to the world for everyone to see. We can believe that His Word and His presence will heal all our infirmities, diseases, insecurities, shortcomings and faults. After one encounter with the Father, we will never be the same again.

I have learned that when we allow GOD to take us through the process our character is built. Yes, the building of our character can be uncomfortable. To erect any structure, digging and cultivation of the ground must take place. Heavy machinery is needed to dig and pull up the stones and weeds that lie beneath the surface. Afterward, an excavation crew comes in and cleans the site to prepare for the foundation to be laid. After the foundation is laid, there is a waiting period. That foundation must set and become firm enough to hold the weight of the structure that is to be built on it and steady enough to go through hard rains, storms and winter blasts.

It's the same for us. When GOD is building our character, He must dig down into the inward parts of our soul, pluck up the stones of our hearts, and give us hearts of flesh: *"A new heart also will I give you, and a new spirit within you: and I will take away the stony heart out of your flesh, and I will give you a heart of flesh."* Ezekiel 36:26, KJV) These are often challenging times, painful times, exposing times ... reality-check times, if you will. GOD excavates and uproots the hidden things that we have locked away, including the hurt of our past – rape, molestation, adultery, lies, betrayals, departures, principalities and every wicked thing that tries to exalt itself above the knowledge of CHRIST. All of this is part of the process of the struggle.

As I look back on the times I stole to eat, I think of how, ironically, I never in life used drugs; how alcohol was never an issue for me. In fact, I would *act* drunk or tipsy just to fit in with others. How revolting it must have been to GOD that I proclaimed something He never intended me to be! I have to say with joy, however, that He never stopped loving me. Through it all, He was there. His Word, stated in multiple Scriptures, is true: "I will never leave you nor forsake you."

During my times of self-inflicted hardship, I kept believing that one day, things would get better. The only problem is, I believed I would make things better for myself. At this point, even as low as I was, I still hadn't stopped to surrender to GOD. Even after feeling the pull and tug on my heart, I was not ready to give up my worldly life and outlook. I was still waiting on the "big payoff." My time was coming, I was sure of it.

Meanwhile, I was living just like that woman at the well. I had given my body to men who did not deserve it. Even giving my body to one undeserving man would have been one man too many.

While financially strapped. I begin to date this older gentleman who was well off. I figured that all I had to do was date him just until I got back on my feet. I didn't like him and was not attracted to him in any way. But I felt that I had to do what I had to do to come up.

This man drove trucks. My grandmother loved him; he knew exactly what to say to have her eating out of the palm of his hand. I felt in my bones that this guy was wrong for me and that I needed to get away from him. But I couldn't. As a truck driver, he made lots of money. I needed what he had to offer…so I thought.

One day he told me he would pay me to go with him to drop off a load. He promised we would return the same day. As I climbed into the cab of the truck, I knew something was wrong. The knot in my stomach was warning me that I should not go with him. But I needed money, so I went.

Three days later, I was still on the road with him … no change of clothes, no toothbrush, no way to call anyone to tell them where I was. He'd forced himself on me several times. I was in shock. I couldn't believe this was happening to me. What did I do to deserve this sexual assault by a second individual only six or so years after the first? That was the question that hounded me. *This has to be a nightmare*, I thought.

I hated this man. In fact, I wanted to kill him. But what could I do? I needed him to get me back home, needed him to live up to his end of the bargain and give me money for taking the trip. So, I took the mistreatment. I didn't jump out of the cab of the truck and run; I didn't call the police and press charges. I just took the agonizing pain. I was the woman at the well. I was lost, hopeless and afraid. The oil in my alabaster box began to leak.

He did not keep his financial promise. He simply dropped me off, leaving me sore and raw. Hot water and soap could not wash away the filth that I felt, no matter how much I scrubbed. I wanted to burn my skin. I wanted to make it all go away. Worst of all, I was alone. I had no one I could call or turn to. I was pitiful.

Weeks went by. I began to realize that I was getting sick every morning. *This can't be,* I thought to myself. *Please don't let it be what I think this is. Please, please, no!*

Going to the store, I stole a pregnancy test … a test that would reveal to me my worth, my value, my next decision in life, who I would become. How could I be pregnant? By this creep, this lowlife? How could this be happening to me? What was I to do? There was only one thing that I felt I could do. I had an abortion … which, it seemed, represented a shattering of my alabaster box.

As I write out the word "abortion," it sickens me in every way. It hurts to remember that I made that appointment, drove hours away, paid money to end a life that did not ask to be here … all because of the decision that I made on that faithless day. All I could think was, *I don't want anything growing in me that is anything like him.* I had to justify my behavior to keep myself out of a strait jacket.

As I type this I pause, looking at my computer screen for several moments, eyes filled with tears, still in pain from the ordeal. I feel the Lord tugging on my heart, reminding me that He forgave me. There is comfort in knowing that.

There are so many struggles when it comes to the process of GOD. You see, GOD wants to take us to the next level, take us to a deeper depth in Him, but we just don't want to go through any struggles. Today, we live in a microwave society – everything has been made fast, convenient and comforting. We can access the Internet on our computers or smartphones and purchase goods online, and those goods are distributed to us without any kind of struggle. Having been thus spoiled, we don't want to go through the process of waiting. We don't want to experience discomfort. We want everything microwave – style. We don't want to wait on GOD to experience the fullness of His salvation. We don't understand that to get to "suddenly," to get to "immediately," there is a process, and that process is called *waiting*. Isaiah 40:31 shows us that *"They that wait upon the Lord shall renew their strength; they shall mount up with wings as eagles; they shall run, and not be weary; and they shall walk and not be faint"* (KJV). But see, we don't want to wait! We don't even want to exercise the running. We don't even want to exercise the walking. What we want, we want *now*. We want to start at the beginning and – bam! – be at the finish line.

What GOD wants us to do is go through the process. In the process, our character is built. We become mature Christians in the process. We get to where we can wait on Him. We become anxious for nothing. We learn peace in the process. We develop our prayer life. The disciples had to go through a process. They had to toil with GOD and walk with GOD to know the heart of GOD. The oracles of His Word had to be written on the tables of their hearts. Their stony hearts had to be taken out and hearts of flesh had to be placed in them. Just as GOD had the prophet Ezekiel to tell the house of Israel, GOD is saying to us that He wants to take away our stony hearts, and give us hearts of flesh. We receive that heart of flesh by allowing Him to make us new, by allowing Him to transform us from the old man to the new man. But, again, there are struggles in the process. JESUS Himself dealt with these, as His very emergence through 42 generations proved out. And He knew, when He left the throne of glory, that there were going to be struggles. Think of the times He told those He'd healed and delivered not to reveal who He was. I believe He wanted to proclaim that He was Lord of Lords, that He was the Great I Am, that He was JEHOVAH. But there was a predestined time for Him to reveal this JESUS had to struggle through the pain to get to the cross.

If we want to be identified with Him and realize the fullness of being made in GOD'S image, we must go through the struggle … a struggle that for many of us begins with merely being called a Christian, as that name often elicits ridicule and mockery from those in this world. There's a struggle in being called a child of GOD, in being called one of Abraham's promises, in being called one of the seeds of Abraham. Yes, there's a struggle in the process. I just don't understand why we don't want to go through the process. We were transformed from the old man, through which we committed adultery, fornicated and did other worldly things. We allowed the enemy to have his way … and even endured a struggle in that! It was a struggle to hide things. It was a struggle to keep our sins from being exposed.

It was a struggle to manipulate and to get over. It was a struggle to come up with schemes to make sure no one would find us out and see us for who we were. It was a struggle to hide text conversations on our phones via secret apps; to change the names in our contact list; to erase our call history and search history so that we could go undetected. But when it comes to GOD and Kingdom building, we don't want to go through the struggle. We don't want to go through the process of GOD changing us and making us new. There is growth in the process. There's growth in the natural; humans grow from an embryonic state to come into this world, then grow from infants to toddlers to children to youth to adults. There must be growth in the spiritual too. And even when we grow in the natural, it doesn't *feel* like we're growing! That's why GOD says we should not be moved by our feelings or emotions. What we should be moved by is the very essence of faith. Faith is the substance of things hoped for. It's where we hope to grow in grace. It's where we hope to be like Him. It's our faith that moves mountains. This is what I found out: The devil isn't necessarily after our bodies, our families, our jobs, our cars or even our spouses. I once heard televangelist and Bishop T.D. Jakes say that what the enemy is after is our faith. When he attacks our faith, he attacks the very substance of everything that we believe in. He attacks what our minds conceptualize about GOD. He attacks our very foundation. That's why GOD tell us not to be moved by fear, by what we see, or anything else except the report of the Lord. It's our faith in GOD that makes us who we are. Our faith keeps us together and keeps us strong. It becomes our identifier, our personality, our speech.

It's our faith by which the Lord is moved. I know people who say He is moved by our tears, but He's not. In the Bible, He wept when Mary and Martha underwent the ordeal of their brother Lazarus' death. But the story was an example to me – and I want it to be an example to the rest of the body of CHRIST – that JESUS is absolutely moved by our faith. He is moved by the revelation of faith in our beings. He's moved by us believing and speaking His Word. That is what raises Him up from His throne to come to our rescue … our quoting the Word back to Him! We say the Word. We believe in the Word. We walk in the Word. We trust the Word. We live in the Word. We don't take anything but the Word for truth. When we do that, we successfully navigate the struggle of the process.   I lacked this faith during my long-ago ordeal: It was very painful to go into that clinic, have that abortion all by myself, sign my name on a form and know I would have to leave a part of me there. But I was so hurt and so violated by what had happened to me. I was young, couldn't even support myself, and had no way to provide for a child at the time. And I just dreaded having to deal with my attacker ever again. That's what made me decide to do the unthinkable. That's one of the things I want to tell women who have taken the same path. Just because you have gone through this doesn't mean you're in it alone ... and it doesn't mean GOD will not forgive you for this atrocity.

Abortion is a horrifying decision to make. At the time, many women feel that it's their only way out of their problem. And the thing I never wanted to do was look at the faces of my children and feel disgust because of their father, so I just didn't know what else to do. I didn't have the foundation to rely on and pull from GOD; at that time, I was going on my own mind and my own thinking. But GOD is a faithful GOD. He doesn't hold things against us. He carried that innocent baby right to heaven, nurtured him or her, and has forgiven me for all I've done. But the hardest thing for me to do was forgive the man who assaulted me. The ironic thing is that I ran into this man when I was working on my last job, which was at a hospital, and attempted to make small talk. He was crippled from his illness. It took everything in me not to spit in his face, give him a roundhouse kick, curse him out and tell him about the hell me took me through. But at that very moment, I saw the love of GOD and how He forgives us for the things we've done against Him. Therefore, I knew I had to forgive. I knew I had to leave myself available as a vessel through which he could receive help. I had to give him direction. I had to show him the right way to go instead of treating him like he treated me, instead of violating him like he violated me, instead of walking away and leaving me the way he left me – desolate – and taking value from me. I had to treat him the way that GOD, and JESUS, does us. GOD looks past our faults, sees a need and meets us where we are. He delivers and sets us free. He engages us, pulls us out of the muck and miry clay, sets us on high again and strengthens us. He helps and forgives us. And that's what I had to do at that very moment – forgive this man for what he had done instead of clutching a mental invoice, instead of remembering what he had done and making him pay for taking something only GOD can give back to me.

At that very moment, I had to forgive. So I did. See, it's the struggle of the process. When we go through the struggle, we must know that GOD is in the struggle. In the third chapter of Daniel, we learned that Shadrach, Meshach and Abed-Nego refused to bow to Nebuchadnezzar, the Babylonian king in whose country they were captives but had achieved positions of honor. When the king made an idol of gold and decreed that at the sound of music everyone had to kneel and worship the idol, these three young men chose not to do so. They chose to believe that GOD was the only wise GOD. They chose to go against a nation and a people who did not believe or trust in GOD. They began to stand together and say, "For GOD I'll live and for GOD I'll die. The only GOD I shall kneel before is the only GOD Who sits in heaven." When they declined to obey the rule of the land and were thrown into the fiery furnace (verse 21) – GOD came through for them! The thing we must remember about GOD is, He is omnipresent. He is a very present help in a time of trouble. He is present in the destruction. He is present in the turmoil. He is present in the struggle. He is present no matter where we are and what we go through. He has already worked those things out. He's already made our crooked places straight. He's already brought things back into alignment with Him because He's already there. So even when Shadrach, Meshach and Abed-Nego were thrown into the fiery furnace, GOD was there. GOD met them in their trial. GOD met them in their pain. GOD met them in their faith – they'd declared that even if GOD didn't save them, they still chose bowing to Him over bowing to an idol. The three young Hebrew men didn't let their circumstance sway them. They weren't moved by their situation or their emotions.

They weren't moved by their struggle. They were moved by their faith. They believed GOD was able to do exceeding abundantly above all that they could ask or think (Ephesians 3:20). They continued to stand on GOD's Word. It did not matter what the circumstance was. It did not matter what came against them, or what appeared to prevail. What mattered is what GOD said. Because they believed what GOD said, GOD gave them victory. When the young men were in the fiery furnace, they encountered a fourth Person who looked like GOD, who WAS GOD (verse 25). He is the "I am that I am." He is Alpha and Omega. He is the beginning and the end. He is the Way, the Truth and the Life. He is ... He is ... He is! If we could only believe that He is with us in our struggle! If we could only believe that He's with us when we go through our depression. If we could only believe He's with us even through the abortion. If we could only believe He's with us even through the divorces. If we could only believe He's with us even through the rapes. If we could only believe He's there with every pain! All we have to do is trust and believe. All we have to do is continue to walk by faith. All we have to do is continue to call on Him. All we have to do is continue to trust in Him. All we have to do is continue to pull on Him. All we have to do is continue to believe. All we have to do is continue to get in His Word. All we have to do is continue to have a relationship with Him. All we have to do is continue to run to Him, our refuge. All we have to do is continue to run to that secret place. All we have to do is continue to believe that He is a rewarder of those who diligently seek Him.

Let me tell you something else. There's trouble when you mess with a child of GOD. There's trouble that comes for you when you try to dig a hole for one of GOD'S children. That's what happened to soldiers who threw Shadrach, Meshach and Abed-Nego into the furnace and, on orders, made the furnace seven times hotter (verse 19). Whatever ditch you try to dig for someone else, you'd better realize you're going to fall in it! The Bible says it's better to hang a millstone around your neck than to cause a child of GOD to stumble (Matthew 18:6) because He loves them ... them, being *us*. It raises Him off the throne when we call Him and hit that right note ... which is faith. It gets His attention when we call Him and we quote the Word – "GOD, You said ... GOD, You declared ... GOD, You proclaimed ... " He watches over His Word, and His Word shall not return to Him void (Isaiah 55:11) but shall perfect the very thing it set out to do. So you'd better believe that when you mess with one of His, you're messing with Him! Not only did the Hebrew men emerge alive from the fire, their clothes and hair were intact. They didn't even smell like smoke (verse 27). They didn't look like what they had just gone through! It may feel bad when you're pulled away from things you know and are ridiculed and ostracized for believing in what CHRIST says. But you'd better know that when GOD is pulling you away, He's getting you ready for something. You'd better know that when you are pulled away, you need to get down on your knees and continue to not only pray, but praise. If you haven't gone through tribulation, you will ... so store up your prayer and your praise. Then, when you're in the valley, it doesn't matter if you can only say "JESUS!" – you're fortified. You've already stored up timber. You've already stored up power. You've already stored up the anointing. You've already stored up favor. So, when you call on the name of JESUS, the angels start getting prepared. Heavenly chariots with heavenly warriors go out before you. There's restoration, there's peace, there's hope, there's joy. When you call the name of JESUS, that's power! There's a process in the struggle. Think of the process a seed goes through. When the sower goes out to sow the seed, he sows it into ground that has been tilled. The ground must be prepared to embody the seed. It takes time for the sower to get the earth to where it can receive the seed unto itself. Once the soil is ready, the seed is planted, then covered up. It looks a burial, and goes on to resemble a baptism. How many of you know that we must *die* to really live? Yes, we have to first go through a *death* to be birthed, and to grow. The seed, having gone through a ritual that resembles death, stays in the earth for a time, during which it goes through a process. When soil is placed on top of the seed, it impacts it. Pressure is applied to it, making it uncomfortable. The seed goes through its process alone in the darkness; it's desolate. When we go through a process, we, too, are often alone; sometimes, we must be by ourselves in order to grow. We find ourselves in a dry place and it seems like we're not going to be able to make it. But how many of you know that if you *stay* in the process, if you *stay* in the growing times, if you *stay* in the dark places, GOD is going to build you in the dark places, He's going to build you in the dry places, He's going to build you in the process.

Here is where the baptism analogy comes in. As the seed goes through the process, it's watered. When we're watered, we may feel like we're drowning. Everything seems to be about going from one dispensation to another. The process often seems overwhelming. "I'm not able to make it," we my cry out. "I've gone from that dry place to where it seems like I'm being drowned." We can't get our breath. We can't talk or focus. It's more of the process.

Then the sun starts beating down on the seed. The seed goes from dryness to drowning to burning up. But if we just stay in the process, we'll realize that GOD is tearing us down to build us up. GOD is doing a new thing! This is where the Bible mentions transformation – "Create in me a clean heart, O God; and renew a right spirit within me" (Psalm 51:10). In other words: GOD, give me a transformed mind. GOD, give me a new heart. Make me a new creature that my mind will be stayed on You. Again, at this point the earth seems like a microwave burning up the seed. But then the seed begins to burst! So goes the transforming power of the HOLY SPIRIT.

Eventually, the seed begins to morph into a sprout. We human seeds begin to grow into the purpose and the destiny to which GOD is calling us. But wait a minute! You would think that when the transformation comes, we would be a finished product. That's not how it happens. A seed must be planted down deep in order to grow. It must develop roots. We must link up with the True Vine and a foundation must be established for sustenance, for stability, for hope, for joy. The seed can't just shoot up. First, it's got to shoot *down*; the root must go deep into the earth. If you're going to be just a little lily, your foundation, or your roots, will be shallow. But if you're going to be a huge tree that's planted by the river of water, you've got to *go down* to be able to come up. The problem is, we don't want to go down for GOD. We don't want to go down in prayer. We don't want to go down in fasting. We don't want to go down in hope. We don't want to go down in faith. All we want to do is stand up and be seen. Hear our names called. Take the mic as it's passed to us. Collect likes on Facebook. Be Instagram idols. All we want to do is shoot up ... but GOD said we've got to go down before we can come up. So get over yourself, trust GOD and just let Him work. Let Him tear you down and build you back up.

When the transformed seed begins to emerge from the ground as a sprout, there's another process. When GOD builds us up is when the enemy tries to take us out. But GOD said that because we took the time and went through the process, no devil in hell will be able to prevail against us. No weapon formed against us will prosper (Isaiah 54:17). Nothing will be able to pluck us out of His hand. As you shoot up, you begin to give the Lord all the glory. You begin to give the Lord all the praise. Then you go ahead with GOD because you stayed through the struggle of the process.

Chapter 3

Positioned for Persecution

†

If the world hate you, ye know that it hated me before it hated you. If ye were of the world, the world would love his own, but because ye are not of the world, but I have chosen you out of the world, therefore the world hated you. Remember the word that I said unto you; the servant is not greater than his Lord. If they have persecuted me, they will also persecute you, if they have kept my sayings, they will also keep yours.

John 15:18-20, KJV

And He said unto me; my Grace is sufficient for thee: for my strength is made perfect in weakness. Most gladly therefore will I rather glory in my infirmities, that the power of Christ may rest upon me. Therefore I take pleasure in infirmities, in reproaches, in necessities, in persecutions, in distresses for Christ's sake, for when I am weak, then I am strong.

2 Corinthians 12:9-10, KJV

Our position in GOD comes with persecution.

When we look at persecution, we think of JESUS, His Stripes and the Cross. We think of persecution in terms of what our Savior went through.

When we think of the Trinity – the FATHER, the SON and the HOLY SPIRIT – we think of glory, grace, joy and peace. But how many of you know that wrapped in your glory is persecution? Wrapped in your joy is persecution?

But how many of you know that wrapped in your glory is persecution? Wrapped in your joy is persecution? I nee

The thought of being persecuted is, to say the least, not fun. But, I would encourage you to change your perspective for a minute.

There is a position of persecution to which you are being called. And it's right in the center of His Will!

I heard a preacher say that GOD will allow that Pharaoh to harden his heart against you – in other words, He will allow that situation in your life to be insurmountable – so that His glory can be revealed.

GOD will allow a great fish to swallow you whole so that His glory can be revealed.

GOD will also allow a woman to have an issue of blood for 12 long years so that He can heal *her* while on the way to heal *your* dying situation ... in other words, your miracle will be delayed so that His glory can be revealed.

What I have learned is that we want the *promotion*, not the *affliction*. We want the glory but not the story. I hate to break this to you, but it doesn't work that way. As Bishop T.D. Jakes says, all blessings come with burdens. And I want to let you know that with every position there is persecution.

At this point in my life, I had accepted The Lord as my personal Savior. One day, while working as a certified nursing assistant (CNA), I was driving to the home of one of my clients. I was tired and hungry – tired of being in the situation I was in and hungry for something other than food. I spoke these words: "Lord, if You will help me, I will serve You for the rest of my life! If You will make things better for me, I will become a mouthpiece for You. I will say whatever You would have me say." I meant every word of that prayer.

No bells and whistles went off. No confetti fell. No lights flashed. Nothing appeared to change. But the one thing I did know was that my *helplessness* immediately changed to *hopefulness*! My thought process was changing. My stony heart was being replaced with a heart of flesh, as stated in Ezekiel 36:26. My hunger intensified … hunger for something the world could no longer give me. I didn't know how I was going to stop going to the club, stealing or cheating; I just knew that it was over. That life was over. There had to be better for me. No more pain and hurt. Giving my life to The Lord had to protect me from perils of this world.

Indeed, from that point on, the nightclub life I'd so loved lost its appeal. The pain and brokenness of my past began to scab over and heal. The bitterness subsided as a better tomorrow came into focus. I looked forward to what lay ahead of me, especially in terms of a romantic relationship. The next relationship was going to be perfect, healthy, Godly. The right one. Right?

Unfortunately, that was not to be the case.

While singing in the church choir, I noticed a young, very nicely dressed man in the audience who noticed me. I later learned that while sitting there, he pointed me out to his uncle, who was sitting next to him, and declared that I would be his wife. He waited until after church to approach me and introduce himself.

After meeting him, I thought I had hit the jackpot. Not only was he tall, dark-skinned and very handsome; he was intelligent and astute, with the gift of gab and an overall swagger that was enticing.

He immediately informed me that he was a preacher. He was trying to impress me. It didn't work; I was actually intimidated. But there was something about him that drew me to him ... flesh. We exchanged phone numbers and began to date. He did prove to be an anointed preacher.

Soon, he took me to visit his parents. When we drove up to their house, his mother was working in the yard. I began to hyperventilate. His mother was a district missionary and one of the foundational pillars of the national convention of which my church was part. I was like, "Is this your mom? If this is your mom, then your aunt must be the State Mother of the church" (an honored position). These women, whom I knew to be sisters, were well respected in the southern region of the convention. They were known for their anointing and love for GOD. Profound speakers of the gospel, they had jurisdiction over the women in their local churches. I was enamored by this man's spiritual roots. How could someone of this caliber want to date someone like me?

Little did I know that GOD was positioning me for persecution. Eight years of persecution. Persecution that would build my character.

I want to make it clear at this point that this book is not about bashing my former husband. It *is* about me allowing you to see into a situation that I could have prevented had I followed the leading of the Lord and chosen life – JESUS – instead of staying in a fruitless union. It's about how GOD will cover you even when you don't know you need covering.

As we continued to date, I noticed that things were not quite right. But whenever he preached and the power of the HOLY SPIRIT fell, I just concluded that my misgivings were my imagination. I was mesmerized at how well he knew the Word and could deliver it. It was fascinating to watch the hand of GOD rest on him. I was learning so much from him about the Word. However, I didn't notice that I wasn't learning anything from him about the Walk.

Eventually, I was introduced to his siblings. One sibling saw no wrong in him. The other sibling warned me, on a frequent basis, to leave this man alone ... to run, but would not explain why. I assumed this was animosity stemming from their personal quarrels – certainly not because of who he was! I was blinded by the outward appearance, paying no attention to the inner man.

Becoming closer to his mother and aunt didn't make matters any better. The spiritual relationship between the three of us was something I felt I couldn't give up no matter what. I needed them in my life. I had a connection to GOD through them and I was bound and determined that what they had; I would have. They were so full of wisdom and knowledge. I learned from his mother that a woman should love her husband and children with all her heart. "Doll, wait on the LORD. He is going to fix everything," she would say to me. She would also remark, "My son is going to be some kind of preacher for the LORD." I believed what she said. The aunt would tell me, "Follow leadership! The men of GOD belong to GOD and He will make everything right. Let GOD handle it. Don't you try to handle it."

These ladies took me under their wings and raised me spiritually. How could this not be my destiny?

Meanwhile, the courtship would go perfectly for a while, but there continued to be those times that were off. Really off. For instance, all I watched on television were the Christian shows on Trinity Broadcasting Network; he would visit my house and tell me that people were going to think I was crazy if I didn't watch something else. He made the same remarks about the open Bibles I had throughout the house and the fact that I did nothing extra-curricular outside of church and only listened to gospel music.

"Run!" the one sibling continued to insist. Again, I couldn't understand why this was being said … or maybe I didn't *want* to understand. This man could preach fire down from heaven! It had to be me who was off; not him.

We married soon after we began dating. The Bible tells us that it is better to marry than to burn (1 Corinthians 7:9). Yet another thing that had struck me as off is that he didn't seem to care anything about this scripture. The more we saw each other, the more the flesh reacted. So I knew that if I wanted to be a part of this family and not "burn with passion," I needed to do the right thing: accept his hand in marriage.

I need to make one thing clear before going on any further. I absolutely do not regret this union, as two beautiful children resulted from it: my son, Jeremiah James, and my daughter, Victory Marie-Divine. They simply prove the grace of our Father. And my ex-husband was not a tyrant; he was an out-of-control addict.

The marriage was blissful for a short season. I grew closer to my husband's family and was settling into my new life. We moved into his deceased grandparents' house, where the rent was free and the utility costs were little to nothing.

I soon found out I was pregnant. Excitement and fear crept in at the same time. I prayed that GOD would not allow this child to be a girl. I did not know how to raise a girl, or have a relationship with her. I feared that I would neglect and mistreat her. I didn't want her to feel how I had felt coming up: lonely and overlooked.

But then, another source of fear manifested. One day, my husband failed to return home from work. The day turned into night, night turned back into day, then day was night again. Hysterical by this time, I called my mother-in-law ... who didn't seem to be alarmed. "Go through the storm," she told me. I was like, "What? What storm? Is he okay? Something has to have happened to him!" Nobody was alarmed except me.

After several days, he came home. There was a stench on him that I had never smelled before. It was a horrible, stale smell ... my idea of what death smelled like. I was confused. What was going on?

My husband's disappearances continued, keeping my stomach in knots. I lived in fear of the unknown.

Then came the day, still early in the marriage, that I had to have emergency surgery. I was rushed to the neighboring town. My husband told me that, while I was in surgery, he would go home, gather a few of my essentials, and immediately return. Seven days later I was still in the hospital ... and he had not returned. I was more concerned about him than I was myself. But those feelings of concern would shortly come to a halt. And the street life that I had left behind would come creeping back up in my rearview mirror.

My parents drove two hours to visit me in the hospital. Questions concerning his whereabouts began to flow. I could tell that my mother, a no-nonsense person, didn't buy the lies I was selling her; however, she didn't pry.

As I lay in that hospital bed, crying and in excruciating pain, I knew I was in for a journey that I knew nothing about. One thing I know to this day is that it was only GOD who kept those voices in my head from manifesting into personalities.

My husband never returned to the hospital. As it happened, the same sibling who'd warned me about him was the one who picked me up when I was discharged. I was confused and bewildered. The 40-minute drive home felt like a lifetime.

As we pulled up to the front door and stepped up to the front porch, I had a creepy feeling inside, one akin to desolation. I felt a rush of heat and knew there was something quite wrong.

Sure enough, the unlocked door revealed a home that looked as though it had been ransacked by a band of thieves. TVs were gone. Jewelry was gone. Clothing, furniture and even the air conditioner was gone. The washing machine remained, but there was a dolly underneath it, as though someone had prepared it for removal.

Who could have done this? This was horrible. I felt violated, then angry, then enraged. The urge to go into fight mode returned instantly. Whoever had done this horrendous thing to us was going to pay ... I wasn't going to wait on GOD to avenge us.

The next words I heard knocked me off my feet. "I told you to run and get as far away from him as you can," my sibling-in-law said. "*Now* look."

Could it really be that my husband, my protector, was the one responsible for this?

I ran to his mother. "Doll, go through the storm," she advised again, after which I felt defeated, but encouraged. I stayed with her for a time, as I needed someone to take care of me. She nursed me back to health. Every day she would speak life into me. I watched her pray and speak the Word. I could feel her trust in GOD. I could feel my faith increasing. My spiritual house was being cleaned again. I could feel the shift from one level to another. A realignment. A repositioning. A transformation. GOD was taking me from milk to meat. He knew exactly what I needed.

There I was … married to a man who was an amazing preacher. As we'd come to know each other, he'd taught me the Word and taken me to church with him every time the doors opened. As his wife and an aspiring missionary, I would accompany him on his various engagements, watching the spirit of GOD come into the sanctuary whenever he preached.

But at night I would have to hide my purse and all my valuables from him to keep him from stealing from me to buy crack cocaine.

I had been positioned for persecution.

Let's look at this word "position" for a moment. When GOD positions you, He is planting you. He is rooting you where He has placed you.

How do we become rooted? See, when GOD positions you, His intent is for you to become stable and mature, wherever that position happens to be. That way, when the finished work that is you comes forth, your foundation is steadfast and unmovable. That way, when persecution comes, you will be able to *stand* rather than acting in an undisciplined or immature manner … whether that involves posting rants on social media, slashing tires or getting your gun. It is embarrassing to see the behavior of the undisciplined and immature!

When you are planted or positioned, you will feel as if you are being smothered. You are being buried, dying, if you will. It's during these times that we pluck ourselves up, aborting the process that GOD is taking us through in our lives. We don't like to feel the discomfort of going from milk to meat. Also, we don't want to be *hidden* while our relationship with GOD is developed based on prayer, praise and persecution. (You see, GOD will isolate you to ill-u-min-ate you for His purpose.) GOD will conceal you from the enemy as well as yourself and the world. You don't understand why no one is taking note of what He has placed inside of you. Little do you know that He is concealing you not only from the enemy but from you! During this period, you will be hidden from everyone else as well. This is the time you will begin to doubt your existence and your purpose. But if you can wait on due season, He will reveal your destiny.

Many of us have celebritized our walk with GOD so much that our relationship is based upon how many likes we can get or how many times our post has been shared. And we scatter at the first sign of a storm, as the Bible says in Mark 4:17: "And they have no root in themselves, but endure for a while; then when tribulation or persecution arises on account of the Word, immediately they fall away" (ESV). We didn't allow Him to develop us in the secret places of Him; therefore, we weren't positioned for persecution.

Colossians 2:6 says, "As ye have therefore received Christ Jesus the Lord, so walk ye in Him: Rooted and built up in Him, and stablished in the faith, as ye have been taught, abounding therein with thanksgiving" (KJV). When you are rooted, you are suited!

Let's look at David for a second, David was a shepherd boy out in the field, minding his own business, when GOD sent Samuel to anoint him as the next king of Israel. David is said to have been 15 years old when GOD began positioning him to becoming king. But he was 30 when he was finally anointed as king. During his wait to rule, he had to endure much persecution from King Saul, who wanted to kill him. Have you been despised because of the call GOD has placed on your life – a calling or a position that you never asked for, and never pursued? You never cut anyone down so that you could be on top. From your standpoint, all you've done was serve and love GOD. But the call is evident on your life. You may not be able to see it, but others do … and they will try to block you.

But know that what GOD has for you, is for you! The Bible declares that your gift will make room for you and bring you before great men (Proverbs 18:16). And Deuteronomy 28:2 assures you that "all these blessings shall come on thee and overtake thee, if thou shalt hearken unto the voice of the LORD thy God." (KJV) All you have to do is allow Him to prepare you in the secret places of Him and mature you through whatever persecution comes.

Psalm 91:1 tells us that "he that dwelleth in the secret place of the Most High shall abide under the shadow of the Almighty." GOD goes on to tell us in verses 14-16 that because we love Him, he will deliver us; He will set us on high because we know His name. When we call on Him, He will answer. He will be with us in trouble. He will deliver and honor us; satisfy us with long life; and show us His salvation.

There is a secret place, or secret position, in GOD that will allow the persecutions to come. How do we react when it does? We take on the attitude of Job: "Though he slay me, yet will I trust in him … " (Job 13:15).

While David was being persecuted, he never retaliated. He knew that GOD saw what was being done to him. But he didn't allow that persecution to hinder his relationship with GOD.

Exodus 14:14 says, "The Lord shall fight for you, and you shall hold your peace" So why is it that, at the first sign of external trouble, we turn away from our Eternal GOD? Don't allow the troubles of this world to drive you away from Him; allow them to propel you toward Him! Remember Paul's words in Philippians 3:14: "I press toward the mark ... " Toward the mark … T*oward the mark!*

In the book of Genesis, we find Joseph the Dreamer, also positioned for persecution. It was his "pit experience" that prompted him to seek after GOD the more. It was his pit experience that anchored him for promotion. It was during his pit experience that the immature boy transformed into the immeasurable man.

Joseph, Jacob's favored son, was betrayed and thrown into a pit by his jealous brothers because of something over which he had no control (except, perhaps, for blabbing to his brothers about those symbolic dreams involving them bowing down to him).

Sold into slavery by his brothers, Joseph achieved a trusted position in Potiphar's house, until Potiphar's wife – whose romantic advances were rebuffed by Joseph – lied on him, claiming he'd tried to sexually assault her.

(Have you ever been lied on? Have you ever questioned GOD when there is one bad thing happening after another? 1 Peter 4:12 says, "Beloved think it not strange concerning the fiery trial which is to try you, as though some strange thing happened unto you" [KJV]). Joseph did not allow his external circumstances to turn him away from his ETERNAL GOD!

There is an anointing that comes from persecution. We don't know what's in us until pressure is applied. We are like olives. The website Scribblenauts.wikia.com describes an olive as "a small oval fruit with a hard pit and bitter flesh. Green when un-ripe and brownish black when ripe, [it's] used as food and as a source of oil." Without pressure being applied to the olive, the oil can't come out. When pressure is applied to us, and we are able to withstand, the fresh oil of the HOLY SPIRIT runs from our hard and bitter flesh. Then we are able to praise GOD through the good times and through the bad, as indicated in 2 Corinthians 4:8-9: "We are afflicted in every way, but not crushed, perplexed but not driven to despair, persecuted but not forsaken, struck down but not destroyed!" Likewise, 1 Peter 4:16 says that "Yet if anyone suffers as a Christian let him NOT be ashamed, but let him glorify GOD in that name" (ESV), while 1 Peter 3:14a assures us that "even if you should suffer for righteousness' sake, you will be blessed" (ESV).

Our greatest example of one who suffered persecution with grace was our LORD JESUS, who while on the cross, prayed, "Father forgive them, for they know not what they do." (Luke 23:34a, KJV).

Being positioned for persecution doesn't mean GOD is singling you out to pick on you (or allow you to be picked on). He doesn't wish discomfort, inconvenience, pressure and pain on His children. But it's through those things that we are strengthened in Him … and He is glorified.

Chapter 4

Stay in the Fight

†

A Psalm of David. Blessed be the LORD my strength, which teacheth my hands to war, and my fingers to fight:

Psalm 144:1, KJV

One of our most common weaknesses as people of GOD is our lack of knowledge of how to stay in the fight. We look at fighting in the natural realm and not in the spiritual realm. The reason we don't know how to fight in the spiritual realm is that we don't know the Word of GOD. We don't know how to fight *spiritually* because we don't understand the concept of fighting in the *spirit.*

Second Corinthians 10:4-5 tells us that our warfare is not carnal but mighty through GOD, to the pulling down of strongholds. Here, the Apostle Paul is making the point that we tend to conceptualize fighting physically instead of fighting with prayer. We have traditionally fought with our hands, our finances, our intellect, our education. We've fought from the perspective of what we think should be right according to the natural realm.

But GOD does not work in the natural realm. He works though His Word. He wants us to fight by faith. He wants us to fight by His will. He wants us to fight by calling on His Word, calling on his name, and believing that He is able to do exceedingly abundantly above what we can ask or think according to the power that works in us (Ephesians 3:20). He does not want us to fight physically, because our bodies get tired. (Even JESUS got tired when He was on earth.) But GOD keeps our inner man fueled up: "Therefore we do not lose heart. Though outwardly we are wasting away, yet inwardly we are being renewed day by day" (2 Corinthians 4:16, NIV). And whereas this flesh will die one day and go back to its original origin – dirt – the spirit man will live on and return to Him: "And the dust returns to the ground it came from, and the spirit returns to GOD who gave it" (Ecclesiastes 12:7, NIV).

As I think about the fight, I reflect on my old "fighter" tendencies. In the military, you're trained to have a mindset to kill. You sign your name on the dotted line saying, "I will kill someone so that someone else can live in freedom. When there's an adversary that is approaching me, I will defend myself, my country, and everyone in it." You are given weapons and taught how to use them. So, when I was discharged, I was different. I wasn't a pushover anymore. I'd learned how to use my hands. I'd learned how to maneuver and strategize. I'd learned organizational skills. I'd learned all the things that would enable me to outthink an opponent and win a battle.

This training came in handy when I went nightclubbing. The persona I took on was akin to a spirit. If a confrontation sprang up, especially one that involved one of my friends, I'd handle it. I did not play! I'd even put on a little weight because I wasn't going to let anybody push me around. If anybody was going to be thrown around, it was going to be the other person, not me. While the other person was talking – or screaming – I wouldn't say a word. I was too busy planning to outmaneuver and outthink that person. That's how the enemy is. He's strategic and cunning: "Your enemy the devil prowls around like a roaring lion looking for someone to devour" (1 Peter 5:8b, NIV).

Thinking is not what GOD wants us to do when we're in the fight; He wants us to *believe*. He does not want us to *strategize* when it comes to the enemy; He wants us to *trust*! GOD wants us to know what the enemy is capable of, but He wants us to trust in Him and what He is capable of. We have to know that this fight is already fixed. We must know that GOD is the beginning and the end, the Alpha and the Omega. He is in Genesis and Revelation at the same time, He was, and is, and is to come! JESUS has already won the fight for us, given us the blueprints and the cheat sheets. We already have what it takes to be more than conquerors in this world.

But the enemy tries to sell us lies, of course. When those lies are heeded, doubt comes in. When doubt comes in, fear comes in. When fear comes in, we've already lost the battle.

GOD is calling you to another level in Him. He's given you a measure of faith (Romans 12:3). Faith is where you get your sustenance. It's in faith that you can simply *speak* to a mountain, ordering it out of your way, instead of *climbing* the mountain. GOD didn't call you to be a mountain climber; He called you to put on faith, along with love, joy, hope, peace and kindness. He called you to *speak*. He's given you a word to proclaim, declare and decree. He called you to stay in the fight! He called you to make sure that whatever you do for Him will last. That's part of the harvest from which you can pull.

Staying in the fight is where your self-worth is. That's where your victory comes in; that's where your value is; that's where your sustainability is.

Growing up I watched my mother, before she met my adoptive father, fight her way out of a lot of situations. There were relationships she went through in which she had to defend herself. There were times where she defended my siblings and me as well. She didn't allow anyone to mess with her children!

I'd also mentioned that, growing up in grade school and middle school, I was bullied. This was such a horrible experience. Being bullied is a violation of one's self-esteem. It strips you of courage and births insecurities and self-loathing. It makes you compare yourself with others. It makes you try to create a carbon copy of someone else's life instead of being satisfied with GOD'S perfect blueprint for you.

I've heard all my life that hurting people hurt people. This is a true statement. This is why bullies exist. They transfer their pain to the next person. And being bullied birthed anger in me. I came away from the Armed Forces with fighting "in my blood." I was a ticking time bomb. To call me out of my name, especially the "b" word, was a clear indication that you wanted to have a confrontation. Matter of fact, if I so much as heard through the grapevine that someone was talking about me, I would assault them … no questions asked; no conversation made. I didn't walk away from anything or anyone.

Of course I had to undergo a huge attitude adjustment to allow GOD to fight my battles for me. There is a trust factor that comes into play. Learning to depend on GOD to fight for me, when I was so used to fighting for myself, was horrifying … at first. As I got into the Word, I began to see that GOD'S assurance that He will fight His children's battles could be found throughout it:

Don't repay evil for evil. Wait on the Lord to handle the matter. (Proverbs 20:22, TLB).

As I was with Moses, so will I be with you; I will not fail you or forsake you. (Joshua 1:5, RSV)

The Lord will fight for you, and you won't need to lift a finger! (Exodus 14:14, TLB)

Do not give punishment for wrongs done to you, dear brothers, but give way to the wrath of GOD; for it is said in the holy writings, punishment is mine, I will give reward, says the Lord. (Romans 12:19, BEB)

Turning my will over to GOD has saved my life. It has kept me from jail and hell.

Not only was my former husband abusing drugs; he physically abused me. Well, let's put it like this: We fought. I sure don't want anyone to think he just jumped on me; I wasn't having that.

I remember an instance in which we were having one of our altercations; if I remember correctly, I was around 5 months pregnant. Enraged, he held me down and whipped me with a belt. My dislike of him at that point bordered on hate. Drugs, poverty, betrayal, neglect and now this! I wanted him to suffer as he caused me to suffer. *He was going to pay*, I'd decided. (Mind you, I had given my life over to CHRIST at this point and was an avid speaker for Him.)

Night after night, I pondered how the repayment for his actions would be served. It had become an obsession. It was all I thought about. To look at him turned my stomach. I could not wait for the day he felt the same pain that I felt. At this point, my alabaster box was broken. And oil was gushing out of the broken places.

After my son was born, we moved from my husband's hometown and returned to the city where I had grown up and attended school. My sister, who has always been a protector of her siblings, opened her doors to us.

One evening, after one of his binges, my husband was relaxing on the couch, unaware of my plan for revenge … and unaware that I'd decided it was time to carry it out. I went into my brother-in-law's closet, retrieved his belt, and told my sister to follow me. I went into the living area and started to beat this man with the belt. As I beat him with all the fury from the pain he'd inflicted on me, I thought it would make me feel better. It didn't. I actually felt foolish. But I didn't stop. I was trapped by my own lust. … not sexual lust, but the lust of doing what I wanted, making my own futile decisions. I'd even lusted after GOD instead of loving Him. I'd been approaching Him in necessity instead of in reverence. I had fallen and didn't realize it. Evil for evil was my goal.

As I look back, there were so many ways that I was in breach of my covenant with GOD. But thanks be to GOD, and the fact that nothing can separate me from Him – neither death nor life, neither angels nor demons, neither today's fears nor any worries about tomorrow; neither the powers of hell nor any power in the sky or on the earth …nothing! (Romans 8:38-39).

Staying in the fight is not operating independently of GOD. It is operating in tandem with Him. There is never a situation He wants you to handle on your own. He does not want premeditation of sin. He desires that your whole heart be dedicated to following the instructions laid out by His Son!

Psalm 34:17-18 declares that when the righteous cry out, the Lord hears them and delivers them out of all their troubles; and that the Lord is near those who have a broken heart and saves those with a contrite spirit. And what I have truly learned is the reality of 2 Cor.10:4-5 – that we don't fight physically; our weapons are "mighty through God to the pulling down of strong holds ... and every high thing" that tries to exalt itself above the knowledge of GOD.

The enemy studies our weaknesses and aims for those things that are low-hanging fruit, or easy access. He watches our every move, learning which situations we handle ourselves and which situations we allow GOD to handle. Those that we tend to handle ourselves become the more breachable areas of attack. He looks back in our history devising a plan of attack using those very things and/or people that are the closest and most dear to us. He knows what will make us anxious, and therefore he conspires to manipulate us into forgetting what the Word says – to "be anxious for nothing, but in everything by prayer and supplication, with thanksgiving, let [our] requests be made known to God" (Phil. 4:6).

This is when it is imperative to stay in the fight, remaining in your position in GOD. The darkest hour is just before dawn. The enemy is quick to present an illusion of defeat to get you to despair. The plan is to get inside your mind, take control of your thoughts and cause you to give up looking for dawn: *I see no change, so why continue? GOD can't be listening. Why would a good GOD continue to allow this to happen to me, happen to my family, happen in the world? He must be asleep!* If the enemy can get you to give up instead of enduring to the end, you will miss out on GOD's best for you.

GOD desires us to take His Word for truth. He instructs us in Psalm 62:5 to wait quietly before Him, for our hope is in Him. 2 Samuel 22:3 says that "my God is my rock, in whom I find protection. He is my shield, the power that saves me, and my place of safety. He is my refuge, my savior, the one who saves me from violence" (NLT).

GOD is calling for you to stay in the fight. Know that He is fully in control of every situation concerning you. You have to be fully persuaded to stay in the fight.

Whether it's illness, divorce, depression, abandonment, poverty, or prejudices that you are battling, GOD has not called you to give up the fight! In Him, we are overcomers and more than conquerors.

Staying in the fight, which is not carnal (even though at times, we fight dirty), requires the correct armor ... also not carnal. Ephesians 6:13-18 exhorts you, the believer, to

> **... take unto you the whole armour of God, that ye may be able to withstand in the evil day, and having done all, to stand. Stand therefore, having your loins girt about with [the belt of] truth, and having on the breastplate of righteousness; And your feet shod with the preparation of the gospel of peace; Above all, taking the shield of faith, wherewith ye shall be able to quench all the fiery darts of the wicked. And take the helmet of salvation, and the sword of the Spirit, which is the Word of God: Praying always with all prayer and supplication in the Spirit, and watching thereunto with all perseverance and supplication for all saints. (KJV)**

Let's look at these pieces of armor individually.

The **belt of truth** is what holds us together. It's our stabilizing force. Truth keeps us balanced. That truth is the Word, whole and honest. Our breastplate of righteousness is supported by the belt of truth; without truth, our righteousness is like filthy rags in GOD's sight. The belt of truth must fit our spiritual frame; it can't be too big or too small. It must be designed by GOD for us … His truth, His brand, His label.

I struggled because I wanted to make *my* thoughts *my* truth. I wanted what I said or thought to become law. I felt as if my sin was not as deadly as my ex-husband's sin, so I drove (pushed) him with what I called "truth," causing more harm than good. My problem was not knowing when to "shut my last mouth." My mouth was so bad that when I closed one, there was still one speaking because I had to be right all the time, and not allow a word in edgewise. I was plucking my house down with my bare hands (my mouth).

The **breastplate of righteousness** is designed by GOD for each of us, born of CHRIST'S sacrifice: "For He made Him who knew no sin to be sin for us, that we might become the righteousness of God in Him" (2 Corinthians 5: 21, NKJV). Your breastplate of righteousness is tailored to fit you. GOD knew what you would go through and what you would need. He designed your breast-plate to protect your heart and your soul.

What I found myself doing was trying to be the gauge of righteousness for my ex-husband. That was truly my problem. I based his righteousness on a comparison to *my* righteousness instead of the righteousness of the Father, which is based on love and forgiveness. I felt that if my husband was not living what I deemed as right, he would forever be indebted to me. I "invoiced" him for every wrong thing he did to me … which turned my "righteousness" into filthy rags.

The **preparation of the gospel of peace** is, as explained in the New Living Translation, "the peace that comes from the Good News so that you will be fully prepared." The Bible says in Hebrew 12:14 to "follow peace with all men, and holiness, without which no man shall see the Lord" (KJV). We must have a readiness for peace. A readiness to stand on the Word. A readiness to be an imitation of CHRIST. Paul said in 1 Cor. 11:1 to follow his example as he follows that of CHRIST. Elsewhere in the Word – Psalm 37:23 – it says that "the steps of a good man are ordered by the Lord."

I wish I really had committed this Scripture to heart instead of merely committing it to memorization. To know is to do. I followed peace with no one during these times. I was mad at the world, and especially mad at my husband. I wondered how he could do such unthinkable things, then act as if nothing was wrong. I allowed myself and my situation to disrupt my peace. I lost so much of me back then; so much of me that I will never be able to replace – but GOD has done so!

The **shield of faith** is necessary for survival; Hebrews 11:6 tells us that "without faith it is impossible to please him: for he that cometh to God must believe that he is, and that he is a rewarder of them that diligently seek him" (KJV). The first verse of that chapter defines faith as "confidence in what we hope for and assurance about what we do not see" (NIV). Faith, in computer terms, is our motherboard. It's our protection against the enemy's fiery darts. Stripped of faith, we're left to our fear and, well, we know how the enemy can exploit our fear!

I had no faith; I was spiritually naked. My faith was ripped from me as a garment. I was never prepared. It left me open and venerable. Surrendering my faith was like removing my vision. I was blinded and lost, walking in fear. I had no hope. This caused me to become jealous when I saw others with active hope. Without faith, I began to age more quickly.

The **helmet of salvation** protects our mind and thoughts. Our mind is our headquarters; to use a little computer-ese again, it's our database and our drop box. It's where we receive and disseminate spiritual information. Ideally, the HOLY SPIRIT lives here. The helmet of salvation would be the enemy's next target, once the shield of faith is compromised. If the enemy captures our mind, he has the rest of our members. No amount of armor can protect us after our mind is seized.

The single most dangerous thing I ever did, even more than participating in the drug trade, was live a double-minded life. Listen, when you are double-minded, people hate to see you coming. You can't be trusted. You can't trust yourself. You will get to the point of almost hating yourself. This is where the suicidal thoughts come in; life loses its worth. I had to become committed to living … and fast.

The Word of GOD is a tool of both defense and offense. "Swords were used to protect oneself from harm or to attack the enemy to overcome or kill him," according to an article, "What is the sword of the Spirit?," at Gotquestions.org. "All Christian soldiers need … rigid training to know how to properly handle the Sword of the Spirit, 'which is the Word of God.' ... We know from 2 Timothy 3:16–17 that the Word of God is from the Holy Spirit and written by men. Since every Christian is on the spiritual battle with the satanic and evil forces of this world, we need to know how to handle the Word properly." What did JESUS use as a defense when the devil tried to tempt Him after 40 days in the wilderness? The Word. What do we use when going on the attack against the devil in areas – geographical and societal as well as spiritual and mental – that have fallen in his hands? The sword of the Spirit.

Just like the misuse of an actual sword can be dangerous, misusing the Word is treacherous ... more so, actually. I have heard so many people mishandle the Word and use it for their personal gain or for influence. In my ignorance, I would use the Word out of context to prove my point to my husband. Every time I did this, I felt the discontentment of the HOLY SPIRIT. I found myself working in witchcraft and craftiness. Manipulation of the Word for selfish motives is dangerous. I quickly corrected these actions, as I did not want to suffer the spiritual consequences. I would warn every reader: Don't take advantage of the knowledge of The Word! GOD will not be pleased.

Fueling it all is prayer. As a preacher once said, prayer is a pre-emptive strike. Prayer is not just a ritual in which we ask GOD for stuff! It's a tool by which we achieve intimacy in our relationship with GOD. The Bible has plenty to say about prayer, including Paul's admonishment to "pray without ceasing" (1Thessalonians 5:17). Even the secular world acknowledges benefits of prayer. According to "10 ways praying actually benefits your health!" (thehealthsite.com), prayer takes away stress, makes us less likely to be depressed; protects us from stress-related sicknesses and lengthens our lives. It's by prayer that we receive not only spiritual nourishment in which to stay in the fight, but instruction from the HOLY SPIRIT Himself as to how to be victorious.

So again, I say ... stay in the fight. GOD has given us too much ammunition to lose, including Himself!

Chapter 5

Reaching for Better by Faith

†

I press toward the mark for the prize of the high calling of
God in Christ Jesus.

Phil. 3:13b-14, KJV

We members of the human race desire better for ourselves in one way or another. It's certainly been the
case with every person who has ever shared their
dreams and goals with me.

Merriam-Webster's online dictionary defines "better" as an ad-
jective which means "more attractive, favorable, or commendable," "more advantageous or effective" and "improved in accuracy or performance."

There is something that is intuitively hard-wired in us that drives
us, as children of GOD, to reach for the manifestations of the
Word. Paul, by his own stated actions, encourages us to forget
about those things which are behind and press towards those
things which are before, saying, "I press toward the mark for the
prize of the high calling of God in CHRIST JESUS." There is a
mark that we should constantly strive for; and that's CHRIST.

Forgetting those things that are behind is a prerequisite to moving
or reaching forward. I have found that you can't move forward
by looking, or dwelling, on and in the past.

This was certainly a struggle for me at one time. It seemed as if the more I wanted to forget the past and press forward, the more I was distracted and railroaded by my tainted past.

I would suffer the most from these overwhelming thoughts whenever I was asked to speak or teach. During this time of study and preparation, I would mentally be ripped nearly to shreds by thoughts of my past ... my indiscretions and insecurities. The one thing I realized was that I feared success. See, I was more comfortable with failure. It was my norm and my language. I communicated through failures. I feared the fall that might come with success. I felt as if I could not live up to any area of my life except for that of being a mother. This is why I accepted the bare minimum that life had to offer.

Looking at me, one could not detect this deficiency. But it was quite evident. Only those who I let in could see it; however, I never admitted or acknowledged it. I think it's why I've always had a heart for the less fortunate, those who needed help ... "projects," if you will. I had this innate ability to believe GOD for *their* success, but not for my own. It was not until others saw things in me that I clearly didn't see, and told me about these things, that I became empowered to believe GOD for the unthinkable. I am now convinced that GOD deals with us in our inability ... our deficiencies. It's then when He gets the glory.

Speaking of His glory, we as a human, finite-minded race are glory seekers. I realized this when I went from one extreme to the other and found myself *still* in a struggle that prohibited me from reaching for better by faith. The more success came in my ministry and in my secular work, the more I had to learn humility. Glory seeking is a tool the enemy uses, especially against those who have self-esteem issues. Glory is sought by those seeking to fill a void. A microscopic examination usually reveals some past event that tore a hole in the soul of the one who so thirsts after affirmation – glory, if you will. (This is why you must be filled with the HOLY SPIRIT. He will bring you notifications and downloads that reveal the enemy's tactics and will strategically direct you so that you can avoid pitfalls. If you *do* fall, He is there to raise you up and get you back on your feet.)

But I had the hardest time forgiving myself for the sins of my yesterdays, even *with* the baptism of the HOLY SPIRIT. I could be in the middle of a wonderful interaction with Him in church service – my hands raised high, tears flowing down my red cheeks – and an image from my past would suddenly capture my attention. There were times when my insecurity and jealousy would present themselves. This disruptive thinking would interrupt my worship to the point that I had to declare what the Word says: "There is therefore now no condemnation to them who are in Christ Jesus, who walk not after the flesh, but after the spirit" (Romans 8:1. KJV) Over and over and over, I would have to make this decree, otherwise my thoughts would leave me upset and discouraged.

It bothered me badly to go from worship to begging for forgiveness for sins for which GOD already forgave me. It was easy for me to forget the everlasting covenant of JESUS CHRIST when the mental attacks bum-rushed me. What I learned from this experience was that the enemy was trying to get me to throw in the towel and stop going to church services. What I had to do was to keep going, even when I felt defeated. I had to realize that my flesh does not rule my spirit; rather, my spirt was the ruler and authority of my flesh.

The enemy doesn't want us to walk in the freedom and liberty of GOD'S Word. If we stay "bound" by what we are free of, we are never actually free; we are living beneath our spiritual privilege.

Our covenant, or contract, with GOD doesn't bear any small print. It wasn't written for GOD to gain access into our lives by force. It was written for us to have access to Him freely. Oftentimes, contracts in the natural come with fine print and stated in language that is confusing and sometimes disadvantageous to stakeholders. This is not the case with our Father. He makes His covenant so plain that even no one need err.

Reaching for better by faith involves our laying hold of GOD'S Word and committing it to memory so that we can operate at our fullest spiritual potential. Committing the Word to memory doesn't mean memorizing every Scripture to sound spiritually intelligent or manipulating GOD or His people with our emotionalism. It means memorizing the integrity and character of GOD so that we can be doers of the Word and not hearers only. Some of us know the Word by memory, but not by statues. We know how to recite it, but not how to *live* it. We can judge *others* by it, but not judge *ourselves*. JESUS says to remove the beams from our own eyes before trying to remove motes from the eyes of others!

When are we operating at our fullest spiritual potential? When we use faith as our currency to function in the Kingdom; to realize the promises of GOD. Just as money is the world's currency and is used to buy and sell, faith activates the plan of GOD to bring us to the "expected end" proclaimed in Jeremiah 29:11.

Let me see if I can make this a bit clearer. Faith is the substance of things hoped for and the evidence of things not seen (Hebrews 11:1). Faith is what we need to receive the things desired of GOD, and the proof that a thing will come to pass! Faith moves the hand of GOD, who delights in our trust in Him. He loves proving

Himself faithful. When we pray His Word and believe that what we are praying for will come to pass, He watches over His Word to ensure that it doesn't return to Him void or insufficient. There are no "hot check" promises from GOD. He is El Shaddai, the All-Sufficient One!

1 John 5:14 says, "And this is the confidence that we have toward him, that if we ask anything according to his will he hears us" (ESV). One fundamental truth we must understand: What we pray for must be according to His will. It has to be what He has ordained for us to be, and have. JESUS instructs us to pray, "Our Father which art in heaven, Hallowed be thy name. Thy kingdom come, Thy will be done in earth, as it is in heaven" (Matthew 6:9-10).

Reaching for better by faith is a process during which we enter the **Secret place**; we find **clarity**; and we learn to have **joy**.

Let's explore these.

The secret place

The Bible has plenty to say about the Secret Place Psalm 91:1 reads, "He that dwelleth in the secret place of the most High shall abide under the shadow of the Almighty." Psalm 32:7 says, "Thou art my hiding place; thou shalt preserve me from trouble; thou shalt compass me about with songs of deliverance." Psalm 27:5 reveals that "For in the time of trouble he will conceal me in his pavilion; in the secret place of his tabernacle shall he hide me; he will set me up upon a rock." (all KJV).

As women, we are always searching for a place or thing that will take our cares away or give us relaxation. We quote that old bath-product commercial: "Calgon, take me away!" We are looking for something to take us away from our problems, our situations, our circumstances, our depression, our woes, and, for some, even our marriages.

In this secret place is refuge and protection. This secret place is where GOD communes with us and builds our character, changing each of us from the old man to a new creature in Him: "Therefore. if any man be in Christ, he is a new creature: old things are passed away; behold, all things are become new" (2 Corinthians 5:17, KJV). Not *some* things ... but *all* things are become new!

It's in the secret place where your palate is changed to where you hunger and thirst after righteousness, after the Word and after GOD'S heart. It's in this place where the devil can't find you.

Psalm 27:2 says, "When the wicked, even mine enemies and my foes, came upon me to eat up my flesh, they stumbled and fell." Psalm 91:5-8 declares, "Thou shalt not be afraid for the terror by night; nor for the arrow that flieth by day; Nor for the pestilence that walketh in darkness; nor for the destruction that wasteth at noonday. A thousand shall fall at thy side, and ten thousand at thy right hand; but it shall not come nigh thee. Only with thine eyes shalt thou behold and see the reward of the wicked" (KJV).

We want to make our prayer closet the secret place, but I need to let you know that the secret place is not tangible but spiritual. It's the Holy of Holies where CHRIST resides, where the veil is rent. It's that brazen altar, where you offer burnt offerings of sacrifice from your heart. It's where only you and GOD have entry. It's where you open up and give of yourself, where the blood is sprinkled. It's where the commandments are written on your heart. It's where, as Romans 12:1 says, you present your body a living sacrifice, "holy, acceptable unto God, which is your reasonable service." (KJV).

I have to be honest. It's not easy getting to this secret place; this spiritual place. The enemy fights tooth and nail to keep you from arriving in this place of contentment with GOD.

When the enemy is fighting against you and you have taken life's blows, it is very difficult to see yourself as secure and protected. See, this was one of my battles. How could I feel protected when I was constantly in a war zone? How could I feel secure, when my electricity was being disconnected due to nonpayment and it was cold in the winter, hot in the summer? If a bill didn't get paid, where was the security in that? How could I continually believe that things were going to be all right when one day. things were going well and the next, all hell was breaking loose? My life at the time was up and down. A roller coaster. Nothing was ever *stable*.

All I can say is, the devil thought I was going to throw in the towel. The funny thing about it was, GOD kept making a way … over and over and over and over! The more things fell apart, the more He showed Himself faithful. The more I felt as if I was in this alone, the more He showed me He would stick closer than a brother. The more I lacked, the more He showed Himself to be more than enough. I couldn't help but believe that He wasn't having it any other way. He loved me!

It's during times like this that your prayer life is built. It's during times like this that you learn to worship GOD in spirit and in truth. It's during *this* time that ministries are birthed, visions are revealed, and JESUS is manifested. There is forgiveness in this time. There is healing in this time. There is restoration in this time. It's in the secret place of GOD that He reveals Himself to you.

Clarity

Clarity, which Thefreedictionary.com defines as "the state or quality of being clear; transparency; lucidity," only comes from GOD.

1 Corinthian 2:13 makes this point: "Which things also we speak, not in the words which man's wisdom teacheth, but which the Holy Ghost teacheth; comparing spiritual things with spiritual" (KJV). The only way to receive clarity is through The Word of GOD, for "in the beginning was the Word, and the Word was with God, and the Word *was* God" (John 1:1, KJV).

JESUS is our clarity. What I have found is that we want to base our clarity upon our own opinion, on what we think is right – not what the Bible calls truth!

We live in a world where anything goes and where truth is often obscured by confusion. But know that JESUS is the Way, the Truth and the Life; none comes to the Father except Him.

James 1:18 says, "Of his own will he brought us forth by the word of truth, that we should be a kind of firstfruits of his creatures" (ESV). Ephesians 1:13-14 reveals, "In Him you also, when you heard the word of truth, the gospel of your salvation, and believed in Him, were sealed with the promised Holy Spirit, who is the guarantee of our inheritance until we acquire possession of it, to the praise of his glory" (ESV). JESUS is our clarity and ONLY Truth!

Now let's not get it twisted. The devil is not going to sit by and allow us to have clarity and truth, a CALGON experience, without opposition.

Job 2:1-2 lays it out for us: "Again there was a day when the sons of God came to present themselves before the Lord, and Satan came also among them to present himself before the Lord. And the Lord said unto Satan, from whence comest thou? And Satan answered the Lord, and said, from going to and fro in the earth, and from walking up and down in it [seeking whom I may devour]" (KJV).

See, the enemy is crafty and subtle. He doesn't come in an obvious way, he comes as a thief in the night with distractions, disturbances, confusions, commotions, diversions, instability, insecurities, departures, uncertainty, indecisiveness, procrastination, conflicts and disorders. But when you have clarity in your persecution, you will be comforted by JESUS' words in John 10:10: "I am come that they might have life, and that they might have it more abundantly." (KJV). So when the enemy comes in – be encouraged because, like a flood, GOD has raised up a standard against him (Isaiah 59:19). That standard is JESUS.

When life seems to have you down; the bible admonishes you, in Psalm 24:7-8, to "lift up your heads, O ye gates; and be ye lift up, ye everlasting doors; and the King of glory shall come in. Who is this King of glory? The Lord strong and mighty, the Lord mighty in battle" (KJV).

When you don't feel like giving GOD glory; tell yourself "I will bless The Lord at all times, His praises shall continually be in my mouth, my soul shall make her boast in the LORD: the humble shall hear thereof, and be glad" (Psalm 34:1-2, KJV). When the devil tries to bring you negativity, know that "all things work together for good to them that love GOD, to them who are the called according to his purpose" (Romans 8:28, KJV). Be like the Apostle Paul and, per Romans 8:38, be "persuaded, that neither death, nor life, nor angels, nor principalities, nor powers, nor things present, nor things to come, nor height, nor depth, nor any other creature, shall be able to separate us from the love of God, which is in Christ JESUS our Lord" (KJV)

Joy

We must understand that joy is not happiness and happiness is not joy. We get them twisted. Joy is a state of being. It's a resolve. It's a destination. It's systemic. It's complete. It's comprehensive. It runs from the veins of GOD to and through you.

Joy doesn't make you move in haste or make wrong, adolescent decisions. (Pride, happiness and self-gratification does.) Joy makes you stand on the Word of GOD and wait for the manifestation. Joy is matter of fact. It is a destiny. It's who you become. Nehemiah 8:10 says that the joy of the Lord is your strength!

Joy is not predicated on emotions, or situations. Joy doesn't take a back seat to your problems. Joy doesn't make you shout and run around the church. Joy is *why* you shout and run around the church!

As you see, reaching for better by faith requires a combination of both action and waiting … moving beyond the confines of your past while standing still and allowing GOD to build and strengthen you. These two do not contradict each other. In fact, while you're trusting Him, you are still reaching. Stay tapped into GOD and you will achieve better … your life in Him will be "more attractive, favorable, or commendable," "more advantageous or effective" *and* "improved in accuracy or performance!"

We'll look more at faith in Chapter 6.

Chapter 6

Perfecting Your Faith

†

So then faith cometh by hearing, and hearing
by the word of God.

Romans 10:17, KJV

Our faith is perfected as we grow to trust in our Savior. The Bible tells us that GOD has given us all a measure of faith, which indicates that He does not give one more faith than the other. We have the responsibility of growing our faith by hearing it and meditating on it both day and night. Hearing and reading the Word is like nutritional fertilizer. Understanding this allows us to know that our faith has the ability to grow, and remain. Our faith is sort of like conditioning our body when we work out. The same way it takes work and effort to build muscle by taking our bodies through a series of repetitive movements, it takes work and effort to build our faith. When our faith is weak, we must apply the Word repeatedly and target those areas that need the most attention.

This was especially hard for me during several years of my life. One of the reasons was because, as I stated earlier, I would compare myself to others, This is a common flaw among saints and sinners alike, and was certainly another crack in my alabaster box! The Bible says we should sharpen each other; iron sharpens iron. This is the Godly way. But when there is carnality dwelling in your members, it manifests as jealousy and envy.

Comparing myself to someone else was a generational curse. Growing up, I always compared myself to my younger brother. I watched my grandmother as she all but worshipped the ground my uncle walked on while barely acknowledging that my mom existed. In my young eyes, this same scenario was playing out with my mother, my brother and me. Distinguished and set apart at an early age, my brother was very controlled and poised. He was the smart one who seemed to have it all together. My mother seemed to be smitten by his every move … rightfully so, as she was proud of him. I'm not saying that she wasn't proud of all three of us, but he was different. He was her baby boy. There is something about a boy and his mother. I should know; I also have a son.

GOD's calling on my brother's life manifested early. He graduated from the Air Force Academy and is a prominent bishop with a lovely family. I am very proud of him. I have watched him perfect his faith over the years! Whatever he went through, he allowed it to make him stronger, and through this strength he was able to build a true relationship with GOD. But because I lacked knowledge of how to celebrate my brother as a child, I struggled as an adult.

What I have found is if you do not *perfect* your faith, you will not access all the benefits that are afforded you through the redemptive work of CHRIST on the Cross.

Our trials and tribulations define us. If we take on an attitude of defeat, failing to exercise our faith and failing to allow ourselves to become conditioned for the fight, we won't receive the reward we desired!

Perfecting your faith may seem to be very difficult. However, it only involves having a tangible relationship with GOD! It's knowing who He really is and accessing Him through JESUS CHRIST! (I know I made this statement a few paragraphs above, but I really want you to get it!)

JESUS is our access to everything heavenly. The Bible says that the cattle on a thousand hills belong to Him (Psalm 50:10)! This means there is no end to His provision – "no good thing will he withhold from them that walk uprightly" (Psalm 84:11, KJV)

Remember when I said in the previous chapter that faith is the currency of the Kingdom? Look at it like this: JESUS is the financial institution. Don't get me wrong. I'm not trying to get you to lust after JESUS for what He can do. I'm trying to make this as plain as possible. Even the illiterate can understand money analogies!

Faith, the currency of the Kingdom, is a medium of exchange. It is what activates movement to go along with your belief. Faith is not *fiat* currency, money whose value comes only through law or government regulation. It's *representative* currency, backed by the gold standard that is JESUS CHRIST. He is the One who brings value to your faith. He is the One who substantiates your faith. He is the One who pronounces you whole due to your faith.

Dealing with a husband who'd sell everything in the house to buy drugs – hiding my purse every day; suspecting him of cheating – I had nothing built up in my mental savings account. My spiritual oil was seeping out; I was hemorrhaging it quickly. I lacked any will to seek replenishment. I could not be a good mother, daughter, sister or friend to anyone, as I had become an enemy to my spouse. I was drained of all hope and motivation. My faith was failing; but in actuality, I was failing my faith! Let me say that again. My faith wasn't failing me, I was failing my faith!

One might ask, "How do you fail your faith?" By not activating its full potential. By wallowing in sorrow and self-pity and waiting on circumstances to change. I was losing ground and time. I was holding my spouse responsible for my happiness, my joy and my wellbeing. He didn't even care for himself; how could he care for me? I was released from this union many times, but I chose to stay, even though I didn't believe in the marriage anymore. What a dangerous combination! I was just as sick as he was.

The Lord was so faithful during these difficult periods. He would warn me of my husband's upcoming drug binges via dreams. I mean, He warned me each time. A demonic spirit with a familiar face would mock me about what was to happen. I would try to warn my husband, but without success. This is where "my" sickness came in, I would act surprised each time ... surprised that each binge was worse than the last.

As I look back today, I remain grateful that GOD spared my life and my children's lives, and didn't let anything happen to us. His love is indescribable and incomprehensible.

According to Proverbs 24:16 and a popular gospel song, the righteous get up again after repeatedly falling. GOD knows we are finite, flawed beings. Our faith is not perfected overnight ... and guess what; it's perfected only in His Son! We can't do or become anything outside of Him. Perfection in anything takes practice. It's practice that makes perfect. Therefore, when we fall, we *must* get back up. When there is disbelief, we must believe again. When we sin, we must ask for forgiveness and try a second, third, fourth time. When David fell, he got back up and wrote the legendary Psalm 51 ... a beautiful apology for his sins concerning Bathsheba and her husband, Uriah.

Perfecting our faith does not mean we have to be perfect. Striving for perfection comes with remaining in JESUS! The Bible says that He is the Author and Finisher of our faith.

As I wrote this book, I came into the beautiful realization that I am an author. As an author, I took my thoughts and ideas for this book into strategic consideration. I planned its layout. I meditated on how I wanted the cover images and graphics to look, how I wanted my name printed, how I wanted the prose inside to flow (GOD gave it all to me). As the author, I knew I had latitude to make this book exactly the way I wanted it; the best I could imagine. I hired the most gifted editor and publisher. We met and communicated countless times. I invested time as well as finances into this book. I did not stop until it was completed to the best of my ability. I am the author and finisher of this book. I only wanted to produce the best for the reader.

I have these capabilities as a limited being. GOD is omnipotent, omniscient and omnipresent. So when He states that He is the Author and Finisher of our faith, that means He has put His best work forward: His Son, JESUS. He will not stop until He is perfected in us. He only wants to produce the best for us as believers. He sent His Son, and His Son left the HOLY SPIRIT to empower us to be, as Paul wrote, more than conquerors through CHRIST.

Another common struggle we go through comes with not believing we deserve what GOD has for us. We limit GOD with disbelief because we feel we are not worthy of His goodness. We think we have done too much evil to enjoy what He has promised. But His grace is sufficient.

I struggled for years with grace. I didn't believe His grace was sufficient to cover my faults. I felt that was enough to cover me for episodes in my life, but not enough to cover me, period. I spent several years in regret and unbelief. The torment of my past was so overwhelming, it almost made me numb to my relationship with GOD. Preventing His grace from doing what He designed it to do will cause your relationship with GOD to be strained! I would walk into church, raise my hands, shout, praise and front (which means to be fake). I was so far away from GOD. I had no real relationship with Him. I remember yearning for a mentor. I needed someone to talk to about my problems and wondered why GOD never sent anyone. In the introduction of this book, I mentioned always being the midwife but never the wife. What I mean is that I always seemed to be someone else's support system, but that was not reciprocated. I begged for a mentor but to no avail. It was not until writing this book that I realized that GOD Himself is my mentor. He was there all the time. He was restoring me through every break, every crack, every shattered place in my life. He was conditioning my faith, bringing it into perfection. I was still under construction, but knew that He was working a new thing out in me.

It's funny how GOD does things. He will take your weakness and turn it into your ministry. See, it was necessary for Paul to have a thorn in his side. That thorn kept Paul depending on GOD. It kept him kneeling before GOD. It kept him in the presence of GOD, pulling on Him. I, too, have a thorn in my side. My thorn has been necessary. It keeps me rooted and grounded and doesn't let me get in front of GOD. It keeps me humble. It actually "mentors" me through my tough times by causing me to worship. It spars with me when I want to get out of His will. It adjusts my attitude when I think I have arrived. It has helped me through my journey.

"And we know that all things work together for the good to them that love the Lord, to them who are the called according to His purpose" (Romans 8:28, KJV). This is truth! My thorn – my indiscretions – has been used to perfect my faith. I see GOD more clearly. His love is much more tangible, and the aroma of His grace is sweet to my nostrils.

He is perfecting my faith each day!

Chapter 7

Love Covers All

†

*And one of the Pharisees desired him [JESUS] that he would
eat with him. And he went into the Pharisee's house, and sat
down to meat. And, behold, a woman in the city, which was a
sinner, when she knew that Jesus sat at meat in the Pharisee's
house, brought an alabaster box of ointment, And stood at
his feet behind him weeping, and began to wash his feet with
tears, and did wipe them with the hairs of her head, and kissed
his feet, and anointed them with the ointment.*

Luke 7:36-38. KJV

Let's discuss, for a minute, the woman in Luke 7.

This woman was a sinner. The Bible doesn't go into the specific sins she'd committed. But there is no big sin or little sin. *All* sin represents unrighteousness. Everything that is unrighteousness is of sin.

This woman had a plan … to find out when and where JESUS would be. The Word says that when she knew JESUS sat at meat in the Pharisee's house, she brought an alabaster box of ointment. Now the alabaster box held the most expensive oil. That meant this woman had to plan, and work, for the oil that was in her box. Because it was of value, she gave mightily of herself to get it.

The woman stood (or knelt, according to the New Living Translation) behind JESUS at His feet, weeping. Can you imagine this woman weeping when she came into the presence of GOD? See, this woman sought GOD. She sought His face. She wanted more of GOD. She wanted, and planned, to be in relationship with Him. She paid the price. She gave up worldly things, things she'd once felt were valuable, things that had cost her. She gave up the oil in her alabaster box just to be in the presence of GOD. But how many of you know that GOD is not going to allow you to give to Him without Him giving back to you?

As the woman stood at JESUS' feet, weeping, she began to wash His feet with her tears, then wipe them with her hair. Back then, women were not allowed to be in the presence of men. A woman could be stoned to death just for the one act this woman committed. But she didn't let the law stop her. She *broke* the law to get into the presence of the One who came to *fulfill* the law. Her life was of no value if she could not be called among those who were of CHRIST. So, she became lawless so that she could become part of who GOD was.

The Word says the woman not only wiped JESUS' feet with the hairs of her head, she kissed His feet. She was much like the woman with the issue of blood. She knew that if she could just get in the presence of JESUS, she would have peace and deliverance. She knew He could transform her and make her new again.

I think of Psalm 51, where a contrite David asked GOD's forgiveness for his sins:

"Create in me a clean heart, and renew a right spirit within me." David wanted his spirit to be renewed, and that's what this woman wanted. She desired a brand-new life, and she knew the love of JESUS would cover her iniquities, wash her clean, transform her.

The Word now reveals that after the woman kissed JESUS' feet, she anointed them with the oil. The feet are the lowest parts of our bodies. And in those days, in that part of the world, sandaled feet could get very dusty and dirty because people took so many journeys on foot. But the woman was not deterred by the condition of JESUS' feet. Again, she was willing to do anything and everything she could do to bask in His presence.

The remarkable thing is that, as the Pharisees began to judge this woman, JESUS saw their hearts and began to call them out. This woman came into a Pharisee's home and did what the Pharisees weren't willing to do. Now we know how the enemy loves to get us caught up and distracted; the Pharisees aimed to discredit JESUS. But JESUS allowed this sinful, humble woman … a woman who knew that the love of GOD covered all … to come in and be an example. This was unprecedented.

Through her desire to change her life whatever the cost, the woman in Luke 7 continues to be an example for us in the 21st century. How many of you know that when you are desperate enough to be different, you will do unorthodox things? When you know that GOD alone can initiate that difference, you will wake up early and seek His face. You will stay up late to seek His face. You will seek *Him* before you seek likes on Facebook and Twitter. You will tread muddy waters for Him. You will break boundaries for Him. You will go against circumstances, against laws, for Him.

Watching the woman's actions, Simon, the Pharisee host, immediately got on his high horse. In Luke 7:39, he "spake within himself, saying, this man if he were a prophet would have known who and what manner of woman this is that toucheth him, for she is a sinner" (KJV). Now JESUS didn't come to heal the well, as He stated in another Scripture. He came to heal the sick! He came to save those who were downtrodden, beaten and bruised. He came to save the wretched. He came to save those who were lost, not those who were found. This woman was lost. Really, if you think about it, who was the most lost – the Pharisee or the woman? I say it was the Pharisee. It wasn't the woman. JESUS already knew she would be seeking Him. Isaiah 55:6 says, "Seek ye the Lord while he may be found, call ye upon him while he is near." Matthew 7:7 says, "Ask, and it shall be given you; seek, and ye shall find; knock, and it shall be opened unto you" (both KJV). That's what this woman did. She began to *seek*. She began to hunger and thirst after righteousness. She didn't let her past impede her present and her future. She knew there was a destiny she had to get to, and that JESUS represented that destiny!

Knowing what was on Simon's mind, JESUS, in Luke 7:40, "said unto him, Simon, I have somewhat to say unto thee. And he saith, Master, say on" (KJV).

JESUS then launched into a parable in the next verse, which takes us through Verse 48:

> **There was a certain creditor which had two debtors: the one owed five hundred pence, and the other fifty. And when they had nothing to pay, he frankly forgave them both. Tell me therefore, which of them will love him most? Simon answered and said, I suppose that he, to whom he forgave most. And he said unto him, Thou hast rightly judged. And he turned to the woman, and said unto Simon, Seest thou this woman? I entered into thine house, thou gavest me no water for my feet: but she hath washed my feet with tears, and wiped them with the hairs of her**

head. Thou gavest me no kiss: but this woman since the time I came in hath not ceased to kiss my feet. My head with oil thou didst not anoint: but this woman hath anointed my feet with ointment. Wherefore I say unto thee, Her sins, which are many, are forgiven; for she loved much: but to whom little is forgiven, the same loveth little. And he said unto her, Thy sins are forgiven.

I'd mentioned before that even after I'd begun to come into the true knowledge of CHRIST, I would be tormented by thoughts of how I'd been in the past. During the praise and worship portion of church service I would be raising my hands along with everyone else. But flickering on the theater screen of my mind would be my sins of the heart, my sins of disobedience, my sins of omission, my sins of *sub*mission ... that is, my refusal to submit to GOD whenever I was "in my feelings." I felt too embarrassed to face GOD. I could praise Him, but I could not worship. The enemy would try to make me believe that I was the only person with this struggle. Nope. I found out that others had learned to hide their struggles.

But I remember GOD telling me there is therefore now no condemnation of those who love Him (Roman 8:1). And I began to realize that GOD wasn't condemning me – He loved me, and all He wanted me to do was repent. When I raised my hands in praise, it was the *enemy* who would bring back my past, from the out-of-wedlock sexual relationships to my acts of theft. That's when GOD had to remind me to pull down everything that tried to exalt itself above the knowledge of CHRIST – *every* thought. *Every* issue. *All* condemnation. *All* judgment. *Everything* that discredited me. *Everything* that disqualified me. *Everything* that brought me into bondage. *Everything* that had caused me to doubt that I was who GOD called me to be ... the called of CHRIST.

I began to *understand* that GOD so loved the world that He sent His only begotten Son that whosoever believed in Him (and on Him) should not perish but have everlasting life (John 3:16). See, I had to understand that GOD had sent His *best*. He didn't send His "second string." He sent His *best*. He sent the Word ... which, as John wrote at the beginning of his gospel, became flesh and dwelt among us. Consider this: In the beginning was GOD. The Word was *with* GOD, and the Word *was* GOD. And it was already in GOD's plan to send His Son to earth to be wrapped in flesh and dwell among us to bring us back into alignment with Him. So, it was GOD's love that covers all. It's His love that brings us back. It's His love that brings us forth. It's His love that projects us into our destiny.

That's why the woman in Luke 7 sought JESUS. She sought His love, His presence, His forgiveness, His will. She sought broken-down barriers. *She sought the face of GOD.* When you begin to seek the love and forgiveness of GOD – when you begin to understand that you can walk in His presence, in His forgiveness and in His covering – that's when you can learn to forgive yourself. You cannot call things that be not as though they were when you're walking in guilt and condemnation, head down and adopting the gait of someone disgraced. GOD has not called you to walk in that. He's calling you to walk in authority. He's calling you to walk in power. He's calling you to walk in joy. He's calling you to walk in strength. He's calling you to walk in His HOLY SPIRIT.

Having answered that call, you can walk with your head held high, knowing you live and move and have your being in GOD's love – love that caused the blood of JESUS to fall and to cover you.

Thank You, JESUS for Your blood. Thank You, JESUS, for Your love!

Chapter 8

Called to be New

†

For we know that the law is spiritual: but I am carnal, sold under sin. For that which I do, I allow not: for what I would, that I do not; but what I hate, that do I. If then I do that which I would not, I consent unto the law that it is good. Now then it is no more I that do it, but sin that dwelleth in me. For the good that I would, I do not: but the evil that I would not, that I do. Now, if I do that I would not, it is no more I that do it, but sin that dwelleth in me. I find then a law, that, when I would do good, evil is present with me. For I delight in the law of God after the inward man: But I see another law in my members, warring against the law of my mind, and bringing me into captivity to the law of sin which is in my members. O wretched man that I am! Who shall deliver me from this body of death? [It is absolutely ... JESUS CHRIST!!!!] I thank God through Jesus Christ our Lord. So then with the mind I myself serve the law of God; but with the flesh the law of sin.

Romans 7:14-25, KJV

We may be saved, but there is constant warfare going on in our minds. The Bible says in Ephesians 6:12, "For we wrestle not against flesh and blood, but against principalities, against powers, against rulers of darkness of this world, against spiritual wickedness in high places" (KJV). Just because you are saved, doesn't mean that you won't have to go through the process.

Remember earlier, when we discussed the struggle of the process and being positioned for persecution? We all have a process. We allow our external appearances to make others believe we are all right internally. But we shouldn't let each other's pretty clothes and nice shoes fool us. We all must fight daily. Romans 5:12 shows that "Therefore, just as sin came into the world through one man, and death through sin, and so death spread to all men because all sinned. We were all, at that point, cursed" (ESV). When Adam took a bite of that forbidden fruit, we went immediately from life to death. The minute we're born, we begin dying. That's the thing we must realize. Our vision of life is distorted because of our accomplishments, our affluence ... but we die every single day. We all have sinned and fallen short of the glory of GOD, Paul writes in Romans 3:23.

Don't ever think you are the only one warring against the sins of the flesh. As believers in CHRIST, we may feel we are the only ones going through certain situations ... that we are the only ones fighting the sins of the flesh, the lust, the desires of adultery, the desires of fornication, the desires of promiscuousness. The enemy tries his best to puts us in this mental cubicle and cause us to think we are alone in the struggle. You are not by yourself! If you live in a body, you are going to go through a process – a fight between your becoming a new creature in GOD and your remaining an enemy of GOD.

The reason the enemy wants you to believe you're in the fight alone is to that if he can isolate you, separate you from the rest of the flock, so that you will condemn yourself, be too ashamed seek spiritual support ("I'm too old to be going through this." "I should know better." "I shouldn't be here.") and therefore be weakened enough for him to do further damage. I oftentimes see people give up because of an inappropriate relationship with a professor, a boss, a co-worker, a church member, a stranger or a friend. Listen, everybody has done wrong. Don't allow the enemy to isolate you. We all have done unspeakable things in our lives that we wish we could forget. Don't ever think you are the only one!

In 2016, when I was making more money than I'd ever made in my life, my electricity was shut off. GOD had placed me in a new position, but He was also conditioning and disciplining me. I remember driving up to the house and discovering that my lights were off. It was just my children and me at home during this period. They were devastated, but I said to them, "This situation is not unto death. People live this way every night. Thank GOD, we at least have the money to get the lights turned back on." The light bill was about $250; I had $243 in my account. Getting service restored the next day took every dime I had, but I still thanked GOD. It was summer, but He had kept the house cool. It was the same with the refrigerator. No food was ruined or spoiled.

I allowed GOD to show me who He was, even in the midst of lack. That's what He wants to do for us … even when we're at the end of our rope, GOD wants us to trust Him and be made new again. The key to our success in Him is to keep fighting! See, the mind will produce negative images and pictures, and if allowed, the pictures will become the blueprint of our every thought. Thus, satan carries out his plan of defeat and shame; bringing us into captivity to the law of sin and death.

I also want to point out how the mind will play tricks on us. One day while married to my children's father, I was home alone, ironing clothes in my living room. As I ironed, I began to not just talk to myself, but have a conversation with two imaginary people. I don't remember what was said, but one imaginary person began to talk to the other imaginary person. Mind you, no one else was there with me. I immediately stopped ironing and began to speak to my mind. My spirit began to cast down those imaginations and everything that tried to exalt itself above the knowledge of CHRIST. I began to plead the blood of JESUS. I walked throughout the house, calling on His name and decreeing that I had a single mind that was stayed on GOD. I cursed those two spirits that had tried to attach themselves to me, take up residence in my mind, and have conversations. I declared that the enemy was a liar. I spoke those things and I believed GOD. I was not going to allow my mind to be split into three different compartments ... something the devil had tried to do to me before. Whenever things hurt me – rape, betrayal, low self-esteem – I would lock them away in different compartments in my mind and throw away the key. What I came to realize was that when I mentally closed off those hurts in their separate compartments, personalities began to be formed. They began to try to take root. When I was at my lowest, these personalities began to surface and speak to one another. But that was when I saw GOD move! He reached down and pulled me out of this immediately, so the personalities could not take root. That's when I realized that there's only so much damage, abuse, distress and neglect the mind can go through. That's when I realized that I had to begin to make a move for my sanity. I had to fight for who I was and what GOD was calling me to be.

The Lord has a blueprint for our lives. Again, we see this in Jeremiah 29:11: "For I know the plans I have for you," declares the LORD, "plans to prosper you and not to harm you, plans to give you hope and a future" (NIV). But the devil's "end" for us is to keep us stuck in our past. He doesn't want us to be renewed. He wants us to always reflect on things that keeps us in bondage. He tries to distort the images in our minds of who GOD has called us to be. If not careful, the mind will try to produce permanent catastrophic "realistic" stories about our future from all the failures of our past.

The warfare begins in our minds, but take heart – it can end there, too. GOD said that He brings us into a new consciousness of who He is, which brings us into who we are: "For he has rescued us from the kingdom of darkness and transferred us into the Kingdom of his dear Son" (Colossians 1:13, NLT).

That's the reason the Bible says to keep your mind on Him and He will keep you in perfect peace (Isaiah 26:3). That's the reason the Lord says to trust in Him with all that we have, all that we are.

Paul says it best: " … Forgetting those things which are behind, and reaching forth unto those things which are before, I press toward the mark for the prize of the high calling of GOD in Christ Jesus." (Philippians 3:13-14, KJV)

When we allow opposing images to take root in our minds and spirit, they then produce fruit contrary to the Word. They begin to war against, to pluck up, who GOD has "called" us to be.

I remember another war that played out in the battlefield of my mind. I love my children with everything in me. I gave my children to the LORD a long time ago, realizing that they don't belong to me; they were assigned to me before the beginning of time and that I was just their overseer. I knew they were GOD's responsibility, that He watched over them, that He provided for them when I couldn't and protected them from danger. But when they were young, the devil tormented me about my children, telling me how he was going to kill them.

At that time, my husband was stealing to buy drugs … a situation the devil also utilized to attack my mind. There were numerous times that my husband would take the car and I would have to go to the dope house to find him. This happened when I was eight months pregnant with my daughter. I had been on bed rest for the full term of my pregnancy because of complications. My mother had planned a surprise baby shower for me near her house. My husband was supposed to take the last bit of food over to the baby-shower venue before coming back to pick me up. He put the food in the car, left, and sold our vehicle for drugs. I found out something was amiss when a family member called me to say she couldn't come to the shower. Then my mom and others began to call me to ask me where my husband was. I put two and two together.

I was not supposed to drive, but I got in my dad's truck to hunt for my husband. I found two young men driving my vehicle in a rough part of town. I flagged them down and ordered them to get out of my vehicle and take me where my husband was. They did so. Now mind you, I was almost nine months pregnant, but as I said before, I didn't back down from a confrontation!

The irony is that these two young men lived, and sold drugs, in a nice neighborhood. While they were transporting drugs in my car, my husband was inside getting high. All this took place while my mother, my sister and other family members were waiting for him to bring the food, and me, to the shower. The food was still inside the car!

Once we arrived at their house, the young men went to get my husband. He was so high that when I punched him in the face, he didn't even feel it. I put him in the car. Looking back, I wonder why I even bothered; I suppose I was embarrassed. I took him to a gas station and made him go into the bathroom and get himself together before we went to my baby shower. I didn't want my mother and my son to experience any embarrassment or pain.

We showed up at the shower about 90 minutes late. I acted as if nothing had happened, but inside, I was humiliated at being linked with someone who would do something this horrendous. When we allow opposing images to take root in our mind and our spirit, all those feelings of insecurity and worthlessness come back – *I'm not enough. Who would want to stay with me?* – along with the isolation and desolation.

But despite my hurt at this incident, I knew the LORD was with me, continuing to give me strength.

I knew because of what Romans 8:30 says: "And those whom he predestined he also called, and those whom he called he also justified, and those whom he justified he also glorified" (ESV). We must understand that if we've tapped into GOD, we're being called from one dispensation in our life to another. We're being transformed and renewed, no matter how messy things may still be in the natural.

More evidence of this can be found in 2 Peter 1:3: "His divine power has granted to us all things that pertain to life and godliness, through the knowledge of him who called us to his own glory and excellence" (ESV). He takes away all the mishaps, all the things we've done, all the horrible things we've been through, all the things we've brought on ourselves and all the things we fell into unawares … and He calls us to excellence.

GOD the Father said, "I am that I am" (Exodus 3:14). JESUS said that "before Abraham was, I am" (John 8:58, both KJV). We draw our identity, our newness, from all of GOD's "I ams." He has essentially said to us, "I am Alpha and Omega, the beginning and the end. I am who was, and is, and is to come, I am the lily of the valley, the Bright and Morning Star. I am Jehovah Shammah, a very present help in time of trouble. I am Jehovah Shalom, the LORD of peace. I am Jehovah Tsidkenu, your righteousness. I am El Shaddai, the All-Sufficient One. I am Jehovah Sabaoth; I am your shepherd. I am Jehovah Rapha, your healer. I am Jehovah Qanna, a jealous GOD."

Jealous? That's what I love about GOD – He is jealous and want to spend time with me! He doesn't want me to go to anything and anyone else before I go to Him. He wants to spend time with me! He wants to connect with me! He wants to fulfill my needs. He wants to hear my distresses. He wants me to call upon Him while there's still day. He wants a relationship. He wants a covenant vow with me, one that is sealed by the blood of the Lamb. That's what He wants with me! He made me, ordained me, called me, justified me and edified me to be of, and in, Him. He is so huge, you can't get over Him. He is infinite; He is the only wise GOD, our Savior. He is indestructible. He is incomprehensible. He is systemic. He is our everything.

He is the King of Kings, our restorer, our reconciliation. He is the One who renews us; the one who called us to be new. He is the HOLY SPIRIT. He is our beloved. He is the salt of the earth. He is an amazing GOD who has called us to be new in Him. We are to be transformed by the renewing of our minds. We are to walk in newness. We are to believe that He is able to do exceeding abundantly above all that we can ask or think according to the power that worketh within us. As we are broken, He puts us back together again. He loves to work the impossible! He loves to work in the intangible! He loves to work miracles in our lives. He just needs us to have faith.

When we become new in CHRIST, we are new creatures. Our communication is new. Our transparency is renewed. We hang around new people. What I've learned is that we're transformed from lowly buzzards into eagles. We're able to rise above the storm. One of the things I tell my staff at work all the time is, "Don't eat with the buzzards. You never see an eagle eating with the buzzards." The eagle flies above the storm. That's what GOD intends for us to do when we're new in Him –soar above the storm, above the fray, above our obstacles, because our trust is totally in JESUS CHRIST.

Our trust should always be in CHRIST and not in social acceptance.

Let's look closer at our obsession with being liked – actually, our insecurity, manifested in an alternate ego. I often see people posting pictures of their lives on social media in hopes of receiving validation from friends, family and strangers. Been there, done that. Our pages and posts would have others believe that we live a life of bliss!

Now don't get me wrong. You should be grateful for whatever GOD is doing in your life, and you should promote His glory for all the world to see. And by all means, *do* be proud of your family and accomplishments.

I am referring, and speaking, to all the broken people who use social media as a mask behind which they hide their hurt and pain. I am especially reaching out to those who are suffering abuse and neglect at the hand of a spouse, whether that abuse is emotional physical, or both. Those who are hiding their brokenness behind a post, trying to find satisfaction or validation from others because they are not receiving it at home. Those who want people to think everything is okay, when everything is chaotic and dysfunctional. Those who are smiling, but actually crying inside.

Let me dwell on spousal abuse for a minute. When we are emotionally abused, it feels as hurtful as physical abuse. The neglect of a spouse is just as painful as a slap across the face or a twist of the arm. It's the same with verbal abuse. It's very hurtful to hear, "I'm not attracted to you," "You done got BIG! You have let yourself go," "Why don't you do something with yourself?" "Why can't you look like other women? You are skin and bones." Or, "I really don't feel the same way about you as I used to. I'm falling out of love with you."

(My heart weeps just writing this. Even now, I can feel the hearts of the readers. Whew ... this is almost too heavy for me to write. These words are unimaginable but are used every day to hurt and paralyze others. The person saying them doesn't understand what this does, but the enemy sure does.)

The most difficult emotional abuse is the refusal of your spouse or significant other to acknowledge you at all. You fix yourself up to look desirable, but after all that, nothing is said. Not even a fleeting glance comes your way ... unless he or she is accusing you of looking good for someone else. Some of you ladies were wealthy enough to have plastic surgery to lift your breasts, cinch your stomachs and waistlines, and reshape your cheek structure to please your husbands, only to be left for a younger woman anyway. And you feel emotionally destroyed.

Let me warn you that a situation such as this can be a satanic setup to lure you into infidelity. When we find ourselves in a lackluster marriage, we may be tempted to turn to someone or something other than GOD to fill that void. And don't think for a minute that an emotional affair is "safer" than a physical affair. It's just as deadly, often undetectable until it's too late. You are cognizant of the importance of staying faithful to your spouse physically, however, you turn to different avenues for satisfaction. Late at night, when no one else is up, you find yourself on your computer or phone, logging into your secret account or hidden app to get a few moments of another's attention. You wait for that person on the other end to say, "How was your day? I couldn't wait to hear from you. I've been waiting right here for you to log in!" Your heart beats fast as you listen in great anticipation for those next words: "I couldn't stop thinking about you today."

Yes, I know the majority of the people reading this book are Christians, but GOD is calling me to deal with what's real. And what's real is this: If you are not getting attention from your spouse, trust me – the enemy will set you up to get it from someone else.

Back in the day, it was said that the devil only tempts you with what you *like*. That is absolutely not true! He will tempt you with whatever you *lack*. I have seen cases were a person leaves his or her spouse for a partner who's unattractive and overweight. Why? Because of the way that person made him/her *feel*. People are abandoning marriages in favor of partners they've seen only on the Internet because of the way they were made to feel. Hearing that person's voice on the phone, or pull their words and images up on the computer, can be intoxicating. Some people leave their spouses to enter same-sex relationships ... again, because of the way the other person makes them feel. (Yes, that is the reality of the 21st century.)

Whether it's a same-sex or opposite-sex situation, the emotional affair partners in these cases are predators. They are using what they know about themselves, what they like and what others like to prey on them. They become confidants, listening to the marital woes of their prey and offering words of comfort while making mental notes and planning their strategy. The enemy is not playing games. He is playing for keeps.

When I was married to my ex-husband, I had an emotional affair. Things got to the point where I would have acted on my urges if I'd had the nerve. Thank GOD I didn't. Some do. But my sin was no less than the person who had a physical affair.

Let's touch briefly on the effects of an affair. (We will get more in-depth in the next chapter.)

Having an affair – seeking validation from someone other than the person to whom you have given your hand – takes something out of you that only GOD can replace. It's detrimental to your future, to your destiny. It takes a part of your spirit man. Living with that decision is torture. It causes your alabaster box to sustain multiple deep cracks … sometimes holes that hemorrhage your oil at breakneck speeds.

A physical affair may begin as an emotional affair. Sometimes it's born out of pure spite, retaliation for what was done to you. Whatever the case is, the difficulties in your life may cause you to run to the arms of another.

An affair may start off feeling pretty cool – an amazing fleshly experience leaving you feeling all giddy inside. But, when you are the called of CHRIST, it won't be long before you go from feeling giddy to feeling like garbage. Your sin will torment you.

It will keep you up late at night, and wake you up early. The web of deceit begins to entrap and suffocate you. What was once fun and tantalizing is now distasteful and disgusting. You end up hating yourself for your actions and mad at the world because you feel it doesn't understand. As you continue the affair, you feel as though everyone knows your secret and is carrying a stone to throw at you at the first available moment. The voices in your mind speak defeat, telling you that you may as well stay in the situation because it's impossible to break free.

You have nobody to talk to. You fear that anyone in whom you do confide will not understand your situation. They may tell you it's just as easy as stopping… or worse, put your business in the street. (Granted, you must be careful of the secret–keepers you choose. You need someone who may have once struggled with the same sin and who, while reminding you of what "thus saith the Lord," will offer words of love, of understanding, of hope.)

We can even have an emotional affair with the church. Let me explain before you discard my statement. We come to church when the doors open and are the last to leave, but we never experience the fullness of the experience of GOD. We go because it's a religious practice. We know how to *look* the part and *dress* the part, but not *be* the part. Our hearts are far from GOD. We enjoy the emotionalism of the service and how it makes us feel. But we don't allow the fullness of GOD to penetrate our souls. We end up having an emotional affair with Him instead of a full-out relationship with Him. We seek Him when we are hurt, ill or poverty- stricken but neglect Him when we don't seem to need Him.

GOD in turn, is present in every situation, waits up to speak with us, tells us how wonderful we are and how He desires to spend time with us … but we ignore all the magnificent things He does for us daily. We walk by Him acting as if He has done nothing. We despise our spouse for treating us this way, but it's the same way we often treat our GOD! Nonetheless, He is calling us out of darkness into His marvelous light of forgiveness and love. He is calling us to be new. New in Him.

Chapter 9

Keeping it Real, Not Safe

†

Give honor to marriage, and remain faithful to one another in marriage. God will surely judge people who are immoral and those who commit adultery.

Hebrews 13:4, NLT

This chapter is for those who are up to the challenge of accepting me for who I am, allowing me to keep things real and not safe. I would urge you traditionalists and religious people to skip this chapter and go forward to Chapter 10. I would urge the rest of you to continue to read this chapter and brace yourselves for *real* adult conversation.

To the young women who are entering marriage. I say that things may be blissful now. But if you keep living, there will be some rough times, whether it concerns the way you two get along or whether it concerns your electricity, gas, water, cable and phone services being in danger of being suspended. You've got to have an anchor in JESUS in order to be an overcomer. For richer, for poorer, in sickness and in health, you've got to be anchored in JE-SUS. If your husband takes his attention from you or even turns his back on the LORD, you've got to be anchored. When your children act like they have lost their minds and you literally want to pull their esophaguses out, you've got to be anchored! You can make it, because you are not alone. Hold on; trouble doesn't last always. It may last a week, it may last a month, it may last a few years, but it doesn't last always. Nobody knows this better than I.

In the previous chapter, I brought up the issue of spousal abuse as well as spousal neglect, which could result in the one being neglected giving in to the temptation to have an emotional affair, if not a physical one. Now I want to go a little *deeper* into the issue of being with a spouse who doesn't really want to be with you, and the temptation to get attention elsewhere. I am a woman, so I'll address this from the woman's point of view.

There are good sisters primly sitting in churches everywhere, wearing white suits or dresses and white gloves, who are going through this struggle with their husbands.

The reason this chapter is called "Keeping it Real, Not Safe" is because as Christians, we tend to want to play things safe. We know how to act the part, so we do. We know how to lift our hands and exclaim "Hallelujah!" or "Glory!" at the right moments. And we think that because we're doing these things, we're worshipping. Falling tears, speaking in tongues and other acts of emotionalism do not necessarily mean that we are worshipping GOD; for some of us it just means that we know how to play the part better than anyone else. What GOD wants, more than the *motions* of worship, is a broken and a contrite spirit.

I've had my time of going through the motions in my worship. Now, I want to not just go *behind* the veil of the temple to meet JESUS. I want to go *into His actual flesh.*

I once read a book that made the point that the flesh ripped from JESUS' body during his torture and crucifixion was more than just His blood coming out; it was our way into Him. I not only want to go into Him, I want to take us into Him. When we get into Him, He goes into and transforms our darkest places ... places that harbor such issues as those unaddressed, unresolved sexual matters.

GOD meant for sex to be enjoyed in a loving marital relationship in a healthy matter ... husband and wife becoming "one flesh" (Genesis 2:24, Mark 10:8). But this aspect of marriage is a favorite target of the enemy, who loves nothing more than to come against marriages in general.

I'd revealed in the previous chapter that I cheated on my ex-husband by way of an emotional affair. He had stopped wanting to make love to me, and I had stopped wanting him to do so. I have searched for books that would tell me why he didn't want me. Again, we would probably be shocked if we knew how many women are out there dealing with that struggle. I knew a younger woman who'd married a man considerably older than she. As he aged, he became sickly. I can only wonder how his wife dealt with her unfulfilled sexual urges, especially as, some studies have found that women experience increased sex drives as they go into middle age.

Illness is just one reason you may find yourself in a marriage that lacks sex. There's also the obvious: Your husband's attention has been lured away by another individual, or drugs, or alcohol. Being in ministry, I know people married to ministers who are too heavenly for their own earthly good; they no longer bring any romantic excitement into their marriages because they have become "all church and no play."

When your spouse is neglecting you, you find yourself yearning not just for sex; you find yourself yearning for attention, crying out to be loved and admired and validated. If the enemy has his way, you'll seek it from every other source you can find. Even after you leave these extramarital relationships, you may still be miserable because you don't know how to ask GOD for forgiveness. You have continued to be the enemy's helpless prey as he constantly brings your sins to your remembrance, condemning you.

Satan preys on our insecurities, our shortcomings, in his quest to destroy us. He lies in wait for a chance to operate. In the case of infidelity, he may not even bother to offer choice bait. with someone who would not otherwise even appeal to you in the natural, but will As I stated in Chapter 8, he will have the nerve to tempt you appeal to your flesh in this case because you are lonely. If you usually go for a tall cup of white milk, he will present you with a short cup of chocolate milk … and you'll go for it if it contains the "right" ingredient. The next thing you know, you've downed half the cup. "Wait a minute," you say. "I don't even LIKE this type of man. How did this happen?"

Sometimes, a married couple whose flame of passion has burned out will turn to pornographic images, photos and films in an attempt to get that flame reignited. Pornography is also sometimes used as an aid in marriages in which a partner is extremely hard to satisfy (or both partners are). I know a number of couples who have brought pornography into their marriages. While married to my ex-husband, I discovered him looking at it alone. It was not my thing, however my marriage suffered because of it. (I have watched it before and found it to be too much for me to handle. It piqued my interest enough that I knew I could not dabble in it because I would be addicted.)

When you and your spouse introduce this into your marriage, you may think it's cool or exciting. *My husband likes it, I like it and we're not cheating*, you may say to yourself. But know that, at the end of the day, exposing your eye gates and ear gates to pornography is like bringing in another person. And it has the same effect as alcohol or drugs: You may get turned on, but as time goes on, the porn becomes a necessary accessory to your sex life. You'll find yourself not only *needing* it, you'll feel the urge to view raunchier and raunchier images to become turned on.

And we understand that Hebrews 13:4 says that marriage is honourable in all, and the bed undefiled" – that what you and your husband do should be considered a covenant while "whoremongers and adulterers God will judge" (KJV). But we must not take that verse too far. For one thing, the verse means that the marriage should be kept free from whoremongering and adultery – it's not saying that anything you try in the bedroom gets a pass!

"The reason the above text is often misquoted is because people have focused on one small portion of the scripture, "the marriage bed undefiled," Georgia marriage ministers Michael and Wanda Collins write an article at the website Christian-marriage-today. com. "The rest of the text has been ignored. In the article appear other translations that clarify this verse, including The Message: "Honor marriage, and guard the sacredness of sexual intimacy between wife and husband. God draws a firm line against casual and illicit sex."

As is then pointed out in the article, "The writer is warning married believers to respect the marriage covenant by guarding themselves from sexual sins."

Viewing pornography – explicit images of people simulating or committing casual and illicit sex – is, essentially, bringing another spirit into your bedroom. That spirit is the spirit of *perversion*.

When you bring in the spirit of perversion, it will try to take over. You may be tempted to seek sexual pleasure when your spouse isn't there ... in other words, masturbate. The next thing you know, you would *rather* be alone experiencing gratification than experiencing it with your spouse. And, these pornographic filmmakers don't care who, or how many, they bring together in those onscreen beds. Watching a couple, or a threesome, or a group engage in "adventurous" sex acts, you may start to want to know what those feel like, smell like, *taste* like. The lust of the flesh and the lust of the eyes take over and bring on a lying spirit, an adulterous spirit, a spirit of fornication, a homosexual spirit.

Make no mistake, viewing pornography is a gateway to ungodliness!

If you have already fallen into this trap, with your spouse or alone, and are still feeling the sting of self-condemnation, take heart. JESUS went to the cross not just for thieves and liars; He went to the cross for those who committed the unspeakable, unthinkable and unimaginable. There is no pit too deep for you to climb out of. You've not done so much that His blood can't cover you! The Bible says he is Jehovah Shammah, which means "the Lord is there." When you *get* to the pit, He's already there. When you tumble down to the lowest, most desolate part of the pit, you'll see that He's already there. There's no dark place you could travel that is not already covered by the Blood. In Psalm 139:7-12, King David offers a tribute to Jehovah Shammah, writing:

> **Whither shall I go from thy spirit? or whither shall I flee from thy presence? If I ascend up into heaven, thou art there: if I make my bed in hell, behold, thou art there. If I take the wings of the morning, and dwell in the uttermost**

parts of the sea; Even there shall thy hand lead me, and thy right hand shall hold me. If I say, Surely the darkness shall cover me; even the night shall be light about me. Yea, the darkness hideth not from thee; but the night shineth as the day: the darkness and the light are both alike to thee.

You must not listen to the devil when he tries to tell you, "You're too far gone. It's hopeless. They know what you did. They're looking at you. They're talking about you." Look, chances are nobody has *time* to talk about you, and they're certainly not in a position to do so.

Remember the woman in John 8 who was caught in adultery and dragged by the scribes and Pharisees before JESUS while He was teaching in the temple. Hoping to trap Him, the men asked what He thought about the woman's eligibility for death by stoning under Mosaic law. After bending down to write in the dust with His finger, JESUS lowered the boom on His questioners: "Let he who is without sin cast the first stone." Then, He resumed writing in the ground. The Bible says the men left, beginning with the older ones. (I believe they were the ones who'd committed the most sins. That is the part we've got to get to: When JESUS made that statement, there was no one who could cast a stone! So, no one has room to judge you.)

We don't want to fail; that's part of our problem. Every person is going to fail. We don't want to fail, so we don't fail gracefully. We don't want our failures exposed, which is understandable. But our failures are part of our testimony. We overcome by the blood of the Lamb and by the word of our testimony (Revelation 12:11). We overcome by sharing about how GOD has brought us through our failures. That's how we fail in grace. But we don't want to do that. We don't want anyone to know we're not perfect.

When I told people about the contents of this book, some asked me, "Are you going to expose all your dirt? I hope you don't air all your dirty laundry." I said, Wisdom tells me what I need to say." When I was hungry and homeless, I told the Lord, "If You deliver me, I will be Your mouthpiece." I didn't say, "I'll put boundaries on it" or "I'll tell it only to a certain extent." I said, "If You would do what You *know* You are perfect in doing, I will do what I *can* do for You – and that's tell somebody how good You are." A weak testimony is a weak witness. But if you want to let people know you are the product and the proof of GOD'S grace, you will gladly tell your story.

To all the single people reading this book: Everything above still applies. Being single is not the end of the world. Wait on GOD to bring you your Boaz or your Ruth. As I'll explain in the next chapter, waiting on GOD's timing is essential to a healthy, prosperous life.

Chapter 10

GOD's Timing

†

Wait for the Lord; be strong, and let your heart take courage;
wait for the Lord!

Psalm 27:14, ESV

GOD's timing is not our timing. You would think we'd have gotten that by now, considering how often we believers have heard this statement, or the more elaborate "GOD may not show up when you want Him to, but He's always right on time" … and considering the Scriptures that back these sayings up.

Nonetheless, it can be tough to "wait on the Lord." In the world of unbelievers, people make some of their worst mistakes when they try to take matters into their own hands or, in today's slang, microwave their destiny. A woman wants a husband now, so she dates and gives herself to the wrong men. She wants a child but has no husband yet, so she has a child out of wedlock. A man wants to be financially prosperous and it's not happening fast enough, so he resorts to dishonest or illegal practices to speed things up. An employee decides he is not moving up in the ranks fast enough at the company, so he undermines a competitor or even a superior.

But wait – we as Christians seem to want to predict our own timetable, too! We look at our brother and sister and equate our "time" with theirs. If they seem to be advancing quicker than we are, we begin to want to rush what GOD has for us. Even Abraham, the father of many nations, and his wife had problems with GOD's timing in regards to the biggest component of Abraham's stated destiny. He and his wife, Sarah, had to wait 25 years between the time they were first promised a son and the time Isaac was born ... and Sarah was long past the age of fertility when this elderly couple had him! "Is anything too hard for the Lord? At the appointed time I will return to you, about this time next year, and Sarah shall have a son," GOD told Abraham in Genesis 18:14 (ESV) after Sarah laughed at the thought of having a baby in her old age. Years earlier, while waiting for the promise to be fulfilled, Sarah had gotten impatient and urged her husband to sleep with her maid, Hagar. The result was Ishmael, who was not the one destined to carry out GOD's plan for Abraham's seed.

I was just like Sarah, I had to have things *my* way and according to *my* timing. As an alpha female, I had had to make things happen, I always considered myself a mover and a shaker. When things didn't happen according to when I deemed that they should, I was discontent. My insecurities stood strong and sounded loud. Learning to wait on GOD was one of the hardest things I had to do. I was always afraid He had forgotten about me. My problem was that I was viewing Him as if He was like other people in my life who had abandoned and forgotten me. During those broken places of my life, He was with me when no one else was. When my oil was almost depleted, He restored me ... and He continues to do so.

In Isaiah 55, GOD makes it clear to us that He does NOT do things the way, or at the time, that we, His creation, would expect or dictate: "For My thoughts are not your thoughts, Nor are your ways My ways, says the Lord. For as the heavens are higher than the earth, So are My ways higher than your ways, And My thoughts than your thoughts" (Isaiah 55:8-9, MEV). GOD is faithful to bring our requests to pass. However, He does so not only in His way but in His time.

When you try to rush the process of your destiny in GOD, it gets you out of His timing and places you in spiritual shoes that are too big for you. Rushing GOD'S time causes premature and aborted visions. You may be able to handle the situation for a while, but soon you'll wither away like dry grass.

Just as dangerous as moving before GOD's time, is delaying moving when He releases you to do so. I should have left my marriage long before I did, but I felt I could live neither with nor without my husband. I was trying to make a round peg fit in a square hole, and it just didn't work. One way I expressed my frustration was by profanity. The words that I could make fit in a sentence would shame an entire fleet of sailors! I would curse him for breakfast, lunch and dinner, then wonder why things weren't working right in our marriage. It had gotten to the point that I was the abuser, a maniac who had no idea who I was, even though I was maintaining a missionary's license! I thought the cracks in my box were too severe for that box to ever be whole again. Praying and reading the Word were almost a distant memory. I was in constant warfare even with myself.

There was no limit to what my ex-husband would do, or sell, to get drugs. I can't tell you how many times I put thugs out of my cars after my husband sold them to feed his habit. I would go hunting for my cars and find them in the worst parts of town, occupied by men with drugs and weapons. I would run these men down as if I were the police, and put them out of my cars on the spot! My fury made me fearless. Well, *stupid.*

Things got so bad, I literally wished my husband was dead. There's only so much disregard, disrespect, pain and suffering one can take, so I dwelt on how I could make myself a widow and get away with it. (There are some folks who are judging me right now as they read this book. I say to you, TURN THE PAGE, because at the end of the day there is another woman somewhere, sitting on her couch, reading this that is thinking the same thing. Or, there is a woman who is having the best time of her life today, blissfully ignorant of what the devil has up his sleeve to try to bring her down.)

The crazy thing is, I couldn't let my husband go. He was addicted to drugs and I was addicted to the buffoonery. I didn't realize that it was a spiritual stronghold keeping me in this sorry state. I just kept going around that same mountain year after year after year, broken and in pain.

But guess what? GOD *redeemed* my time. The result of all that trial and tribulation was that I gained maturity, wisdom and power. I learned about GOD's personality and about His love. I learned that His strength is made perfect in weakness and that He would never turn His back on me. When JESUS hung on the cross, that was the last time GOD turned His back on mankind. When JESUS said, "It is finished," that meant GOD would never turn His back on me! This was the main source of encouragement I found when I finally got back into the Word. I also found comfort in Philippians 4:6-7: "Be careful for nothing; but in every thing by prayer and supplication with thanksgiving let your requests be made known unto God. And the peace of God, which passeth all understanding, shall keep your hearts and minds through Christ Jesus." (KJV).

But again, so much of the issue of GOD's timing involves our need to wait for it. When GOD requires us to wait longer than we think we should for what He has for us, we become anxious … and impatient … and angry … and irrational … and, ultimately, bitter. We may even become obstructionists when it comes to other people's dreams and purpose! Trust me, all of this may happen without you even being aware.

The Word has much to say about GOD'S timing:

- 2 Peter 3:8-9 – "But do not overlook this one fact, beloved, that with the Lord, one day is as a thousand years, and a thousand years is as one day. *The Lord is not slow to fulfill his promise,* as some count slowness, but is patient toward you" (ESV). I had to trust the process. The process of His timing. It is funny how we want Him to be patient toward us, but we have no patience when it comes to Him. If He said it in His Word, He will surely bring it to pass.

- Isaiah 40:31 – "But they *that wait upon the Lord* shall renew their strength; they shall mount up with wings as eagles; they shall run, and not be weary; and they shall walk, and not faint." (KJV)

- Finally, we are told in Galatians 6:9 to "not be weary in well doing: *for in due season* we shall reap, if we faint not" (KJV)

What we must understand is that our destiny is not predicated on the oil in someone else's alabaster box. (What GOD has for you, is for *you!*) When we are out of His timing, we stop moving by faith and begin to move by sight. We force or manipulate things to bring the promise to pass. When we activate our own fruitless understanding, we get out of GOD'S time.

Proverbs 3:5-6 says, "Trust in the Lord with all your heart, And lean not on your own understanding" (ESV). Moving out of GOD'S timing will cause us to get in financial ruin trying to be like someone else. We buy homes and cars that we can't afford. We buy clothes trying to be a carbon copy of someone else instead of being the original that GOD has called us to be.

Now Habakkuk 2:2 says to "write the vision and make it plain." It doesn't say to write the vision and make your plans. When we start to make our own plans is when we find ourselves in a conundrum. When we start to make our own decisions is when we get frustrated, proof that we put the *promises* of GOD before the *timing* of GOD. When we start creating our own strategies is when we begin to act immature and undisciplined, making decisions that we will regret later. But waiting on GOD will allow Him to craft us and our character at the same time.

See, everything is in GOD'S timing. And GOD will redeem the time – because He *is* Time! GOD will speed some things up and slow some things down to bring you into His time. The steps of a good man are ordered (or timed) by The Lord.

In the beginning was the Word (JESUS), the Word was with GOD and the Word was GOD. And the Word became flesh and traveled through "time," down through 42 generations. The Word left Glory to be wrapped in flesh; lived 33 years in his particular dispensation; was beaten at the appointed time; died on the cross; rose on the third day at the expected time; and sits on the right hand of the Father, creating time – just so that He can bring us into the Promise of His time!

JESUS not only was about His Father's Business, He conducted that business on the timetable His Father decreed.

"Now after that John was put in prison, JESUS came into Galilee, preaching the gospel of the kingdom of God, And saying, The time is fulfilled, and the kingdom of God is at hand: repent ye, and believe the gospel." (Mark 1:14-15. KJV)

And before that, his cousin John the Baptist, operating on GOD's timetable, prepared people for JESUS' emergence: "The voice of one crying in the wilderness, Prepare ye the way of the Lord, make his paths straight. John did baptize in the wilderness, and preach the baptism of repentance for the remission of sins." (Mark 1:3-4, KJV)

Now just think: Had John the Baptist been jealous of JESUS, what kind of mess would that have been? I often wonder whether I could have been entrusted with the Will of GOD in the same way John was. Have you ever seen one person jealous of another – or two people jealous of each other? It's comical, in a sad way. Picture two people with spiritual gifts, both trying to show them off at the same time. I have witnessed instances in which two extraordinary singers were performing in a church choir, one leading and the other ad-libbing, and the one ad-libbing tries to take over and nearly drowns out the lead. What is the purpose of this? The song goes from a beautiful rendition to an incoherent mess.

I also remember church events during which we missionaries would be lined up to speak, one after the other. The result was what threatened to become a competition and had the potential to descend into a mess! This is not how the Word was intended to come forth. Who gets the glory? Nobody!

Speaking of competition, my ex-husband and I were headed to church one night to an event at which I had to speak. I was to be the last speaker in a lineup of about five missionaries. By this time, my husband had brought so much embarrassment on the church with his drug use and resulting behavior, our pastor had "sat him down" – stopped allowing him to preach – and he was jealous of the fact that I was still allowed to speak. I should not have allowed him to push my buttons, but at a stop sign a block away from the church, we got into a terrible altercation. When we parked at the church I got out, distraught with the knowledge that I had to try to change my demeanor and deliver a word to GOD's people. Once inside, I sat on the front row with the other missionaries while my husband showed his nonsupport by going to a seat at the back of the sanctuary. The women before me got up and preached as if the woods were on fire! I sat there feeling heavy and disjointed, knowing I was to go last. It felt like a competition and I felt unfit and unprepared.

Shortly before it was time for me to get up, I felt a tap on my shoulder. I looked around to see my husband. "You better preach!" he mouthed. He was forbidding me to allow someone else to outdo me! And preach I did. I'd let myself not only be provoked into an argument; I'd let myself be provoked into a spirit of competition.

GOD doesn't want us to be jealous of one another and compete with each other. He wants us to celebrate each other for our uniqueness and be willing to submit our gifts back to Him for service to the Kingdom. If it's not your time, don't force it; doing so causes your light to dim.

We learn of several instances in the Scriptures where authorities sought to seize JESUS, but were unable to do so because "his time had not yet come." When GOD's time for His crucifixion drew near, JESUS entered Jerusalem – where many were heading for Passover – on a donkey. Two of His disciples told Him that some vising Greeks wanted to see Him. "But Jesus answered them, saying, 'The hour has come that the Son of Man should be glorified' " (John 12:23, NKJV). He went on to speak of His coming crucifixion and the results that would come from it: "The time for judging this world has come, when Satan, the ruler of this world, will be cast out. And when I am lifted up from the earth, I will draw everyone to myself." (verses 31-21, NLT) Galatians 4:4-5 says: "But when the set time had fully come, God sent his Son, born of a woman, born under the law, to redeem those under the law, that we might receive adoption to sonship" (NIV).

If JESUS had to submit to the Father's timing, so much more do you! GOD has to build your character for the blessings.

When you wait on the Lord, your waiting is not in vain. You will receive instruction and direction. There is fundamental development in His timing; a spiritual foundational structure is being erected. Maturity and wisdom blossom.

Let me share this quick testimony with you. Two years or so before I began this book, a 17-year-old prophecy came to pass. No human prophet or evangelist gave me this word; the HOLY SPIRIT Himself spoke it into my very being. He told me I would not retire from the hospital where I was working. He said nothing else. It was a pretty daunting prophecy, and of course my carnal man took over my thoughts: Was I going to die, get fired or become desolate? I allowed the enemy to try to misconstrue what GOD was saying.

After these horrific images played in the projector of my mind, a blanket of calm came over me. It was as if GOD had laid me down to rest in the green pastures of His Words. At that moment, I realized that He had my very best interest in His hands, and that He was going to make all things new. He was making my crooked places straight.

But His timing took a while. During the 17 years between the prophecy and its fruition, GOD began to do a work in me. Little did I know He was preparing me for the manifestation of relocation. He began opening doors for me that no man could open. It was all by His might! The favor was incomprehensible. He took me from mediocrity to "blessed in the field and blessed in the city, blessed going out and blessed coming in." It was such a disruption, however, that I didn't realize that my prophecy was being fulfilled ... and I initially became angry with Him. Yes – with GOD! (I immediately repented). I was so used to living a subpar life, afraid of better, that when He began to move me into better I became disgruntled and afraid of success. Honestly speaking, it wasn't until GOD began making things uncomfortable for me that I stopped resisting His will. He stirred my comfortable place; my nest. He taught me how to reach for better by showing me, as a child of His, that this move was and always had been a part of His plan for me.

Let's look, in John 5:1-9, at a certain man who had an infirmity for 38 years.

Some time later, Jesus went up to Jerusalem for one of the Jewish festivals. Now there is in Jerusalem near the Sheep Gate a pool, which in Aramaic is called Bethesda and which is surrounded by five covered colonnades. Here a great number of disabled people used to lie — the blind, the lame, the paralyzed. One who was there had been an invalid for thirty-eight years. When Jesus saw him lying there and learned that he had been in this condition for a long time, he asked him, "Do you want to get well?" "Sir," the invalid replied, "I have no one to help me into the pool when the water is stirred. While I am trying to get in, someone else goes down ahead of me." Then Jesus said to him, "Get up! Pick up your mat and walk." At once the man was cured; he picked up his mat and walked. (NIV)

When we think of the word "sickness," a variety of synonyms comes to mind: An infirmity, illness, ailment, disease, disorder, sickness, affliction, weakness, disability, invalidity, feebleness.

The Scripture says that JESUS saw this man ... not that he saw JESUS, but that JESUS saw him! And although the man had stayed sick 38 years, being beaten to the healing pool by those who were quicker on the draw, we can be pretty sure he rejoiced no less when GOD's time for him to be healed arrived!

Another point about GOD's time ... just as we want to rush the good things that have promised us, we often want to drag our feet and delay the unpleasant things we must go through on His behalf, or opt out of them altogether. Let's look again to JESUS' entrance into Jerusalem. Now He set on fulfilling his purpose, even though it was going to mean horrendous torture and a gruesome death. Just because He was GOD didn't mean he didn't feel every sting of His flesh being ripped from His body with the whip. The torture of his beard being forcibly pulled from his face. The crown of thorns piercing His head. The long nails, driven by a hammer to secure His hands and feet to the cross. The added agony of His back, laced with open wounds, rubbing against a splintered cross as He struggled to breathe. Imagine each breath becoming more laborious than the last as JESUS strained against the nail in His feet while trying to remove the pressure on His diaphragm, just to be able to get air in His lungs! See, He was a real man, with real feelings, who had real love for us. Whatever GOD has for us, whatever tribulation we must undergo and by which He may be glorified, it is vital to our Kingdom roles that we do not try to go against His timing.

How do we keep ourselves in sync with GOD? By keeping a Kingdom mindset. Here are some key components of that mindset.

Understanding that your mind must be renewed and transformed. Lay hold of Romans 12:2 – "And be not conformed to this world: but be ye transformed by the renewing of your mind, that ye may prove what is that good, and acceptable, and perfect, will of God" – as well as Philippians 2:5: "Let this mind be in you, which was also in Christ Jesus" (KJV).

Watch what you allow to penetrate your eye gate. Whatever gets into this gate has a straight path to your mind. And remember that for the enemy, your mind is the first area of attack.

Understanding the importance of operating where you are. JESUS only had a trade as a carpenter. He didn't have a doctor of philosophy degree, medical degree, doctor of pharmacy degree, master's degree or bachelor's degree. But JESUS didn't allow insecurity to discourage Him from being about the business of His Father! Don't allow your lack of education or lowly socioeconomic state to cause you insecurity. Work with what He has given you to work with.

Understanding that your gifts are not about you. Whether it's preaching, teaching, prophesying, tongues, singing or playing music, your gifts are a beautiful sacrificial offering that you must give back to GOD. As 1 Corinthians 10:31 admonishes you, "whatsoever ye do, [to] do all to the glory of GOD" (KJV).

Understanding that you should not covet another's gift. Whatever GOD has established in you, you should allow Him to perfect in you. When we covet, we tell GOD that what He has established in us is not good enough.

Understanding that you should not try to force your way into the inner place of your anointing prematurely. Take the time to die in the outer courts … die to selfishness, die to arrogance, die to wanting to be seen and die to wanting to be heard. The enemy wants to get you off your preordained assignment. He wants to distract you with something that GOD is not yet emphasizing in you so that you will miss what He desires to teach you in this season of your life. Bask in the secret places of GOD and allow Him to establish roots in you so that you will be able to stand against the wiles of the enemy.

So how did I finally break free of the hopeless situation that was my marriage … a marriage that was so toxic that I needed healing, not only in my body but in my soul? I began to be obedient to GOD's voice. I began to love *me* more than the drama. Once these things happened, I found it quite easy to walk away.

Even then, however, it took me a long while to heal, spiritually and mentally. The damage was extensive. My children were almost abused due to my failure to leave when I was supposed to have left. I was angry all the time and yelled and fussed at them constantly. They walked in fear of me because I was short-fused about the smallest things. After each outburst, I overcompensated by giving them material things and saying I was sorry; eventually I felt like the proverbial drunk or drug addict who always comes back with apologies after repeatedly hurting or stealing from loved ones. I had turned into the very thing I had walked away from. Not only was my oil seeping out; I'd begun to crack my children's alabaster boxes. This was not supposed to be happening. But it was.

I quickly ran to the supplier of my oil and requested an entire makeover. He began reconstruction and my life made a turn-around. As time passed, my anger dissipated, and things became not just normal, but good. My children were healthy, and I'd gotten to a place where I could communicate with their father without wanting to cause him harm.

Meanwhile, my ex-husband's addiction caught up with him … legally. After three stints in the state penitentiary, he will be up for parole in 2020. He's still an anointed preacher. And my children love him, but they have accepted him for who he is.

Throughout all my years of trial, the one thing I never did was stop going to church. After I had children, it was a must that I ensure that they knew exactly who GOD was, so this was a priority. After joining New Calvary Temple Church of God in Christ after my divorce, I became active again and rejoined the missionary circle. Things were looking up.

One day, needing work on my newly purchased house, I met my current husband. It was about three years after my divorce from my ex. This man was handsome, well groomed, quiet. We fell for each other quickly and our courtship moved at a breakneck speed. We never really slowed down enough to examine the broken places in each other's alabaster boxes.

We married, after which we enjoyed seven years of bliss. This was a wonderful man, a man who loved me, a man who would work his fingers to the bone. If I even thought I wanted something, he bought it for me. Anything I wanted done, he did it. We had problems, just as in any other marriage, but nothing that we couldn't work through. The children were behaving as they were supposed to. Both were doing remarkably well in school, our small construction company was doing well, and I was moving up through the ranks rather impressively on the federal job at which I'd worked for 15 years. Surplus income flooded our bank account on a weekly basis and we vacationed at least twice a year. My ministry work at church was evolving and I was growing spiritually every day.

I finally had the husband, the kids, the white-picket-fence life for which I'd yearned for so many years.

But slowly, things began to shift. I noticed that my husband's personality was changing, and not for the better. He was becoming short-tempered, having outbursts. He was always tired. We'd stopped spending quality time together as we had in the past. I had chalked that up to him working long hours. But then, I noticed that he had stopped contributing money for the bills and, in fact, had begun to ask *me* for money. My once-loving husband began to exhibit an attitude of disrespect for me, and his relationship with the children was diminishing rapidly.

Then the affection changed. I dismissed infidelity, but I knew that something had his attention. And after months went by I eventually began to wonder if, indeed, some*one* had his attention. On Sundays, we would not only fight about his not wanting to go to church, but come close to blows. He began to accuse me of wanting to change him.

Early one morning I remember him saying that he did not believe that JESUS was real anymore; that he was changing his name to Such-and-Such Bey. He had rejected the Christianity he'd once embraced, and adopted the Moorish faith. Not that I have anything against any other religions, but his decision began to split the family.

Even worse, I came to realize that my earthly king, the man I loved, was suffering from some of the same addictions my former husband had suffered. The Lord revealed to me what was going on.

How did I end back where I was with my first husband? How did I end up back in that same position? I just could not imagine what I had done to deserve this.

I remember us sitting on the stairs in our home one night, talking. My husband seemed distant and confused, almost demonic. I knew something was extremely off when he began to speak as though he had no reason to live. Everything had gone wrong and he didn't know how to get back on track, he insisted. I encouraged him as I always had, but this time nothing got through to him. It was like he was an empty shell with no one at home inside. One of the last things he said that night was, "I love you and never meant to hurt you or the kids." I immediately told him to stop talking crazy talk and assured him that everything would be all right. He stared into my eyes and kissed me ... a cold, detached kiss. I was perplexed. What had happened? What was wrong?

We went to bed that night as normal. I got up and went to work the next morning, giving him a kiss on the cheek before leaving the house and wishing him a wonderful day. As was usually the case, we spoke on the phone a couple of times. I got off work before he did, so when my shift ended I picked up the kids, made dinner and reached out to him by phone as I always did. This time there was no response. The kids and I ate dinner. I placed his plate in the microwave and waited for his call. It never came, so I began to worry. I called his mother; she hadn't spoken with him. Trying not to alarm her, I replied "Okay. If he stops by, tell him to call me." She never called, because he didn't stop by.

I became frantic. I called my husband countless times, but he never responded. The calls would go straight to voicemail. I called the police, but was informed that I had to wait until he had been missing for 24 hours. I lay in bed that night, feeling my brokenness resurfacing, feeling my sheets becoming saturated with the oil that was again seeping out of my alabaster box. What was happening? Sleep did not come; I was tormented by the thoughts that were racing through my mind.

I decided I could not let my children know what was going on. So, the next morning, when my daughter asked, "Where is Daddy?", I quickly made up a story that he was away due to work.

Two days went by; I heard anything. Those two days turned into five. Still nothing. I didn't miss a day of work or church. No one knew that I was figuratively dying, inside and out. In that five-day span, I felt as though I had aged 10 years. I did report my husband missing, but the police could come up with no leads. There was nothing I could do except wait … and cry myself to sleep every night.

Several more days slowly passed with no sign of my husband anywhere. How could this be happening to me, to my children again? My alabaster box was empty.

Or so I *thought*.

TO BE CONTINUED IN THE NEXT BOOK ...

BIBLIOGRAPHY

Zavada, J. (n.d.). How Jesus Shocked the Woman at the Well with His Love. Retrieved January 14, 2018, from https://www.thoughtco.com/woman-at-the-well-700205

Olive. (n.d.). Retrieved February 16, 2018, from http://scribblenauts.wikia.com/wiki/Olive

G. (2017, January 04). What is the sword of the Spirit? Retrieved January 14, 2018, from https://www.gotquestions.org/sword-of-the-Spirit.html

Team, E. (2015, March 20). 10 ways praying actually benefits your health! Retrieved January 14, 2018, from http://www.thehealthsite.com/diseases-conditions/10-ways-praying-actually-benefits-your-health-p114/

Better. (n.d.). Retrieved January 14, 2018, from https://www.merriam-webster.com/dictionary/better

Clarity. (n.d.). Retrieved January 14, 2018, from https://www.thefreedictionary.com/clarity

F. (2015, April 21). Undefiled Christian Marriage Bed » Christian Marriage Today. Retrieved January 14, 2018, from http://www.christian-marriage-today.com/christian-marriage-bed.html

ABOUT THE AUTHOR

Renita M. Hoof – evangelist, wife, mother, leader – has been through life obstacles that would have felled many others. She overcame with the one thing to which she holds fast … her love for Christ, who loved her when she didn't love herself.

Renita has been a licensed evangelist for more than 15 years. She also attended Global Impact Ministries and Bible College and graduated with a minister's and elder's license. She is a committed member of her local church, where she is entrusted to lead and work beside some of the greatest women in the world. Professionally, she has worked for more than 25 years in a hospital setting, taking care of others. She also served in the United States Army as an operating room surgical technologist.

A resident of Little Rock, AR, she is currently a director for the largest hospital in her city. She enjoys the support of a loving husband and two wonderful biological children, along with two amazing stepsons.

Renita has learned that the only true and lasting thing in this world is to be anchored in our sovereign, unchanging Father. Her hope is that those who read this book will be strengthened, empowered and healed.